NERVOUS AND MENTAL DISEA:

[No. 79]

DELUSION AND MASS-DELUSION

By

A. M. MEERLOO, M.D.

Martino Fine Books

Eastford, CT

2021

Martino Fine Books
P.O. Box 913,
Eastford, CT 06242 USA

ISBN   978-1-68422-548-4

Copyright 2021
Martino Fine Books

Cover Design Tiziana Matarazzo

Printed in the United States of America On 100% Acid-Free Paper

NERVOUS AND MENTAL DISEASE MONOGRAPHS

[No. 79]

DELUSION AND MASS-DELUSION

By

A. M. MEERLOO, M.D.

1949

NERVOUS AND MENTAL DISEASE MONOGRAPHS

NEW YORK

Foreword

The human mind is characterized by two antagonistic forces struggling for supremacy. This is the conflict between the intellectual components and the instinctive drives, each apparently attempting to achieve dominancy. In some situations the instinctive forces gain control in a way to encourage those individuals involved to gather in groups, masses and mobs. Here the "herd instinct" becomes supreme with the inclination to organize and to follow and obey a leader. In such situations either much good or irreparable harm to society may result, according to the issues involved.

Psychology is the discipline that has the most direct bearing on our daily activities. Its phenomena are ever present in our feeling, thinking and dreaming. However, the ways in which it works and its actual significance are mysterious to the average person, and the language of the learned in this field is mere jargon to the uninitiated. It is unfortunate that it is not better understood by all, and particularly by those whose duty is to make decisions that may threaten the security of mankind.

Many writers have attempted to inform the public on matters of psychology and psychopathology without having the proper training and experience, the result being a flood of books on the market having little value and too often presenting untrue and harmful pronouncements. The human mind is a very complex system of actions and reactions requiring years of persistent study to acquire even a working knowledge of its intricate patterns of expression and function. The average reader is not able, nor can he be expected to be able, to differentiate between the real specialist and the would be authority in psychological science. There is a great deal of psychological knowledge that has accrued without yet having gained its possible applications in society where it would enrich the lives of the people. The problems of mass psychology are complex and do not lend themselves to an early, rapid solution. Some may never be solved, but it is our task to make careful studies and to disseminate whatever knowledge that has been gained about the psychological peculiarities of so called "mass mentality". Dangers in social life cannot be avoided without some idea of their nature. People should be informed about these dangers and taught to understand that individuals possess inborn tendencies driving them into actions that their logical powers of thought have difficulty in preventing.

This is the duty of our psychopathologists who in the past have devoted the greater portion of their time to working with individuals. Therapeutic work with individuals is important, but the person is only a unit in a huge social organism or mass of human beings influenced and moulded by its form and laws. Most of our mental reactions and adjustments are related to other persons in the mass.

Mass psychology should be brought into the foreground for much needed research with special institutes for the study of its unique problems, where all aspects could be analyzed and data accumulated for the direction of practical applications.

In this monograph Dr. Meerloo, an experienced psychiatrist, has presented a large area of psychological and psychopathological import. He has discussed, psychodynamically, the thinking process in all of its various normal and pathological ramifications and special significant functions. The different types of delusion formation, the problems of the masses, mass thinking, and the characteristics of collective action in its many expressions are treated in a most informative and interesting account. His concepts are clearly stated and they bring together a wide variety of facts, theories and constructive ideas that should prove to be thought provoking and a stimulation to additional investigation.

NOLAN D. C. LEWIS, M.D.

Preface

These essays are the reactions of a psychiatrist to fettered thinking. The first draft was written during the dark days of Nazi occupation in Holland, when the iron blows of official "thought control" smashed down on all free cultural discussion. In such an atmosphere, imagine the cathartic value of setting down one's own aggressive reaction on paper, of clarifying—for oneself, at least—why man must resist attacks on mental freedom and civilization or perish.

These days of conquest saw the people of Western Europe turning more and more to American thought, to the pragmatic philosophy of that huge, free land. Long before the two world wars Europe had been overwhelmed by German romantic idealism. With high-flown words and theories that captivated a willing world, Germany went far toward conquering European thought long before its armies annexed its material wealth.

The first essay attempts to show the change in attitude that arose from our need to stem the German impact on our thinking. It started as a series of lectures in occupied territory and developed into an essay on man's fearful groping with the mind in the midst of his expanding knowledge of the universe. The two shorter essays present some practical implications of our deluded attitudes.

Most of these reflections were gathered without benefit of scientific contact, without access to any literature, without the possibility of research or discussion. Yet the very fact that they were born of mental exile may help them to portray more convincingly the spirit of stubborn resistance that filled our hearts in those days. Are we not becoming increasingly aware of the tremendous influence that opposition exerts in shaping man's mental processes and character?

                                                              A. M. MEERLOO, M.D.

New York, 1949

vii

Contents

Part One
Delusion and Mass-Delusion

Contents

Contents

Part Two

Mass-Suicide and Atomic Fear

Part Three

Some Mental Aspects of the Human Animal
(Remaining Young, Walking Erect and Playing Continually)

Delusion and Mass-Delusion

An Essay on the Capricious Thinking
in Man and Collectivity

To be a part of human tragedy,
To know all things so very well,
But still to act against all intellect.

A.M.M.

I. THINKING AND DELUSION

Can we be made to understand what an exciting adventure thinking is? Can we be made to understand at the same time that there is often more wisdom in silence than in endless talk?

We live in the midst of a curious and continuous clash of opinions. Opinions and catchwords do not arise sui generis. We are constantly swayed and subjected to the convincing thinking of others. We are confronted with persuasive editorials. It is almost impossible to evade the suggestive pressures of the world around us.

In this essay I have briefly attempted to place myself outside the tumult of hastening, deliberating and fighting mankind, attempted to answer how men came to accept their fictions, their chaotic notions and ideas.

The Tragedy of Thinking

The realization that our own open mind and brain are not entirely our own is a tragic one. We come to realize that the weighty thoughts with which we attempt to clarify the problems of our time are partially the products of the thinking of others and partially emerge from the unconscious patterns of our own mind. We think and try to become conscious of the world around us but we are not independent in our reasonable existence.

The new psychology has given us many examples of primary instincts and urges which act upon our thinking. There is a close link between thoughts and emotions. A well-known philosopher, spokesman for a sharp-witted idealistic system, once confessed that during the writing of his best theories, he experienced several curious bodily sensations together with accelerated intestinal activity. It was as if his best logic were expelled physically as well as mentally. He functioned best when suffering from a headache.

Man involves his entire body in thinking and involves it in a distinct, personalized way. Some become quiet, silenced and meditative, others nervous, excitable.

This essay is an attempt, from the clinical standpoint, to account for the various influences that rule our thoughts. Delusion and mass de-

3

lusion, suggestion and mass suggestion have to be accounted for if they are to be corrected.

Thought and Delusion

Our first concern is the problem of delusion. The clinical psychology of the nineteenth century attempted to explain delusion as the result of a pathologically changed process of thinking. It defined delusion as an incorrigible error, as an incomprehensible obstinacy of the psyche. The intrapsychic process of delusion, since it was not understood, was written off as inexplicable. Examples of the curious thought pictures of the mentally diseased were cited, which were impervious to outside influence. These patients tried to prove one delusion with another, even more improbable one, and out of the primary error erected an entire delusional system.

The analysis of this delusionary growth process revealed threads of comprehensible thought with, however, a bizarre and incomprehensible superstructure. Many adequately functioning people who show too much concern with themselves often conclude that the treatment accorded them does not do them justice. This common correctible aberration we refer to as "conceit" and "self-centered behavior". Incomprehensible in the delusion, however, was its fixed, incorrigible nature. The delusion seemed to persevere as an impenetrable mental armor. Many psychologists considered this well protected and armored insulation of the delusion the specific pathological process. They defined the delusion as a specific change in the thinking process, in which self-centered evaluations turned into rigid delusions as a result of pathological processes of the brain. In most cases, however, it was impossible to point to the intracerebral deviation.

Affective Delusions

Beyond these pathological thinking processes there is also the formation of delusions due to the impact of emotions, namely, the affective delusions. When the intensity of certain emotions reaches abnormal proportions the thinking processes change. This form of delusion is a more comprehensible one. It is plausible, for instance, that a person under the impact of tremendous fear might think he is persecuted, or that a person in extreme pain and sorrow might consider these punishment for his sins. But even here our understanding is not complete. The reasons for the persistence of fears and suspicions, their incorrigibility and immutability, seem inexplicable. It is as if a strange growth had invaded the thinking processes and distorted them. Thinking is a vivid, moving, dynamic process, changing and adapting in contact with reality. And it is precisely these aspects, this alertness and dynamism, which cease in the delusionary process.

Thinking as Contact with Reality

The animal lives and moves in a passive world. The human being lives and moves in an active world. His senses transmit a passive picture of reality, but from these fragments he structures his own picture of the reality situation. Active and passive reality are interacting, related to each other. Without this interaction man is lost. This creates the constant need for accounting for both realities, for continually gathering new experiences. This constant process of orientation, confrontation and constant contact with reality is evidenced in the erect posture of man. Unlike the animal, man walks erect and faces reality. It is only under these conditions that the continuous interrelationship between the inspecting subject and the object can be maintained. This relationship is the basis for our relative and temporary knowledge.

Thinking is that process which enables us to come to terms with reality. Through trial and error the subject gradually comes closer to the object and both subject and object undergo change as a result of this interrelationship. This dialectic process of interrelated development of man and world shapes the remaining elements of human culture and civilization.

Limitations of the Psychologist

In judging delusions and mass-delusions the psychologist studies the biological phenomenon of human thought, which, at the same time is his own instrument of research. Only one's own thinking can evaluate that of others. It is an unfortunate limitation of the method that one's own thinking might reasonably form the nucleus for further study. The necessary circularity of the operation in the study of delusions, therefore, poses a paradox which in its essence excludes the subject-matter from philosophy and formal logic.

But having faced this, it is not proposed that the subject be dropped here. It has been shown most convincingly that delusion and mass delusion do exist, that they are dangerous and persuasive. The psychological approach, however imperfect, is urgent. Straight human thinking is in danger and will remain in danger until the nature of delusion and mass-delusion is understood.

Philosophy, logic and the science of critical knowledge have investigated man's thoughts since the time of the ancient Greeks. They provide us with a wealth of subject matter, rules and methods which will be valuable in our psychological approach. However, we do not propose only to judge specific thoughts or rules by which "good" thoughts may be told from "bad", but rather to study the process of thinking as such. The subject matter of the psychology of thinking, unlike the science of philosophy, is the science of stupidity, of delusion and illusion, of the capriciousness of thought.

Our Thought is Capricious

During the past few years we have witnessed ages of science and critical thinking melt like snow in the sun as a result of mass feelings. The process was the same as the formation of affective delusions. The sense of reality dwindled before mass feeling and delusion.

Politically inspired fictions penetrate science and philosophy. Systems of thought provide masks and justifications for brute drives and lust for power. We vaguely sense that desire and instinct are masked behind "logic". Mental tricks are easily substituted for "logic" and out of the multifarious logical possibilities we tend to choose those most compatible with our own desires.

How can we be taught to distrust this self-satisfying pseudo-philosophy? How deep is the relation between thinking and lying? We like to impress ourselves with words and thoughts and then to hide behind those very words. The animal is always true in his affections, the human being, however, selects some parts of reality while others, ignored or denied, fade into obscurity. We are forever expressing, hiding, demonstrating, charging, exaggerating and selecting. Much so-called "healthy" thinking hides hypocritical demonstration. And what is referred to as independent thinking is an unconscious transference and reproduction of the ideas of others. Small wonder that we have grown suspicious of "logic", especially when people emphasize their clear and logical thinking.

SECTION TWO

The old logic, the science which first sought to provide us with immutable laws for sound deductive reasoning, was grounded in the conviction that the thought processes were identical in all persons. Even the "possible" fallacies were tabulated and defined. A list of "thou-shalt-nots" was compiled and as long as truth was dumped into one end of a syllogism truth would unfailingly emerge. Socrates is mortal. Thus it was hoped that through discussion differences could be resolved.

In actuality the surface is only scratched. Clear thinking for any sustained period (five minutes, for instance) is rare indeed. But for two persons to hold a clear, dispassionate and mutually comprehensible discussion, which terminates in absolute agreement, is virtually unknown outside the field of mathematics. (And the only reason for the exemption of mathematics is its highly hypothetical nature. It is a question of *if* I have four apples *and if* you have four apples *then* between us we have eight.)

The main single reason that the old logic is of little use in resolving differences of opinion is that there is no sound method of lighting on a mutually agreeable major premise. Aristotle and the logicians of his time were convinced that "all men are mortal" was an immutable truth, whereas we of the modern world recognize that all the data is not yet in. This is not to be construed as a bland dismissal of modern logic, which is even more hypothetical than arithmetic. It simply means that from a hypothetical premise one can draw only a hypothetical conclusion, and human thinking is rarely carried out on that level. The present world is a chaos of conflicting beliefs, not of conflicting hypotheses. It is not a mere question of "all men are mortal" but whether "this is better than that" or "that is strategically unsound" or "he is an evil man". A living logic sufficient for the purposes of psychology must be equipped to deal with moral and qualitative judgments. Not only are ideas subjective but so are the words that express them. The word "evil" alone has a separate connotation for each person who sees, hears or speaks it.

Fortunately, there tends to be general agreement in practice on the meaning of some of our more common words. Webster—or rather the brothers Merriam—define the word "chair" as "a seat, usually movable, for one person. It usually has four legs and a back, and may have arms." Quite involved arguments may be constructed around this definition. Everything seems to be optional except that it shall hold only one person. Is an upended box a chair? We may argue (teleologically) that it is not, because it was not constructed for that purpose, but then neither are those cut-down and upholstered beer-barrels one falls into! Or we may argue (functionally) that anything becomes a chair when it is used as such. This of course immediately involves small tables, foot-stools, radiators and so on. But happily, one may yet use the word chair without running into much confusion. Through common agreement on the worthiness of communication, we let such vague concepts slip into our speech. Now if such an exhaustive quibble can be provoked on the word "chair", what shall we do with a qualitative judgment?

In short, we are poorly equipped for clear thinking. Provided that in some fortuitous manner we are able to arrive at a few truths by the combination of words of uncertain and subjective meaning into sentences, then we have in logic a powerful instrument for the elaboration and perpetuation of those truths. But a conclusion is apt to be as strong as its weakest premise.

In the psychology of delusion, therefore, we are only rarely directly concerned with logic. The deluded person is not necessarily less logical than his more humdrum neighbors. He simply constructs his syllogisms on different premises. I am a Scottie Dog yet my neighbors expect me to stop barking and stand erect. Who is being illogical?

Logical Tricks as Justifications for Our Wishes

Generally speaking, then, a delusion is a conviction that is arrived at not *il*-logically but *a*-logically. It is a false premise. But it is more than that. If it suits me to adopt a false premise it suits me doubly to justify it and hide its origins. We have a natural distrust of ideas which appear to pop out of the void. They leave questions unanswered. We must invent antecedents for our convictions if we are to maintain them. Recognizing the persuasive power of the syllogism, we select from our social environment those falsehoods or partial truths which, when accepted as premises, yield our conviction as an inevitable conclusion.

My wish to convince myself that I am a superior being in matters of intelligence, taste and appearance, might not meet a direct pragmatic test. I may, instead, adopt an attitude of amused tolerance toward my neighbors. I think my attitudes not wholly unbecoming because I am being, after all, tolerant, and further, I am sometimes quite objective and witty about them. Yet I succeed in conveying the impression that my neighbors require tolerance and that I, by setting myself apart from them, do not.

Wishing to exterminate the Jews, the Germans sought to show, through the medium of a quite truthful (insofar as it went) documentary film, that the inhabitants of the Warsaw Ghetto were filthy in their personal habits and not particular about their excretions. The result was revolting "proof" that these people should be blotted from the face of the earth. Not mentioned was the fact that sanitary facilities were withheld and that people were forced to remain, without moving, in certain positions for so many hours that elimination ceased to be voluntary. In short, the premises from which it would inevitably follow that the Jews were unspeakably filthy were deliberately constructed for propaganda purposes. Witness the growth of a mass delusion.

Ogling Reality—The Only Common Concept

The one concept that transcends the thinking of all individuals is that of coming to terms with and confronting the same changing macrocosm. The manner of doing so, however, varies. There is a continuous and reciprocal relationship between thinking and reality. Thinking enlarges reality, the newly conceived reality constructs a new and enlarged system of thought.

Contrary to previous assumptions, thinking is not a smooth, linear evolution of thoughts. It falls back repeatedly into periods of hesitation, skepticism and agnosticism. It experiences crises, develops circularly and spasmodically like all life processes. It is forever moving toward new worlds and new relations. The unstable being is mobile, inconstant in his thinking.

In times of fear and chaos the realization of the interaction of social occurrences and thought is sharper than ever. Withdrawal into a white tower, a thought-shelter, becomes impossible. During the Nazi occupation an anti-Marxist Hegelian came to my consultation hour and complained of his inability to think. His main concern was with distribution and food provision rather than the philosophical article he had intended to write. When I jokingly told him that he was attempting to convince me of the historical materialistic conception of thought, his headache was almost cured.

There is a continual interrelationship between thinking and social forms. Thinking shapes society—society shapes thoughts. Primitive man, by experiencing life collectively with his fellow men, shares with them collective forms of archaic thinking. The collective thinks for him, so to speak. Civilized man has to relearn to think socially again through augmented conscious awareness of his methods of thinking. His failure to do so constitutes his tragedy.

The Evidences

The formulation of a judgment by synthesis of different associations and impressions may be considered a primitive mode of logical thinking.

The judgment, for instance, that this writer is, or is not, talking sense

presupposes certain basic ideas or evidences on which unprovable ideas
may be built (as in mathematics, complex conclusions). Thus, thinking,
with the human being as the engineer, becomes an intelligent construction. Everyone utilizes these unconscious thought constructions of
which analogies and syllogisms are a part.

Conversations and discussions are understandable as long as they
stem from similar premises. The technique of reasoning, however, results in constant error and chaos. Wrong analogies are constantly
drawn.

Circular Reasoning

Man's present forms of aggressive argumentation and verbal seduc-
tion approach the comical. Not only do we pretend not to be aggressive,
we go so far as to assert that our aggression is nothing but a higher expression of civilization. It was precisely this argument that the oppres-
sor of our country (Holland) used against us. While our country was
plundered and our freedom destroyed, the Nazis asserted that we
were being ushered into the European heaven. Most arguments accomplish little beyond stating their own falseness. One supposes what
one has to prove, and reasoning moves in a circle. It is like the story of
the accused dishonest borrower, who attempted to prove before the
court, first, that he had never borrowed anything, second, that he had
received it in bad shape, and finally, that he had returned it long ago
and did not owe a thing.

The premise includes what one wishes to prove (petitio principii).
In the same way, the tyrannical aggressor argued that bombardment of
an open, peaceful, neutral town like Rotterdam was an emergency
measure perpetrated for the benefit of the people oppressed by democracy.

Constant repetition imbues this argumentative sophistry with more
and more suggestive power. The vicious circle is only too well-known.

As far back as Greek antiquity, a clear distinction was drawn between
everyday reasoning permeated with incorrect syllogisms and analogies
and a pure thinking which is conscious of itself and aware of its limitations. The latter produces philosophical derivatives of a qualitatively
superior order. The clear statement of a problem encourages this advanced treatment.

Psychology and Logic

The psychologist is required to familiarize himself with both types
of thinking. He approaches the process of thinking differently than the

philosopher, for he finds that overemphasis on logic weakens man's links to reality. Life is *not* clearly logical and simply determined, for such logic prevails only in the rule-ridden world of the insect. The psychologist cannot subscribe to the superstition of logical thought. Ideas spring forth illogically. Idle play, sleep and other partially-aware states are fertile soil in which ideas germinate. The determination to think logically is not sufficient for production of thought; the mind requires the motoric power of passion to produce. Man opposes logic when he cannot profit from it, hence a scrupulous application of laws of logic is no adequate guide for the solution of life's problems. Logic only assists in the avoidance of major errors. Kant defined comprehension as the solution of a problem to that extent to which it is adequate for our purposes. The logic of the moron is brought forth as unconsciously as the clear systematic thinking of Hegelian philosophy.

The psychologist allows riddles to exist. He opposes the fiction that phenomena demand an immediate explanation. All logical reasoning was produced as much by impressions and suggestions as logical rules. Logic presupposes a world made tangible by hand and idea, a world in need of coordination and selection. Logic can only prevail in a stable world. Life, however, is forever bypassing logic.

Psychology studies the inner and outer conditions which determine thinking. Philosophy concerns itself with the laws of thinking apart from those conditions. Psychology plays a role in those areas where thoughts are still rigidly rooted in the conditions that are responsible for their growth. The psychologist looks upon thinking as a biological luxury largely limited to the human species. Thinking is a curious biological function, an inhibition of vital functions accompanied by a curious self-accounting consciousness. The anatomist Bolk (4) ascribed those peculiar inhibitions and retardations of functioning and the special structure of the brain to the erect posture of man, his long youth and his never-ceasing play. Because man remained a foetus and his physical defenses did not develop and differentiate, as for instance in the ape, his forebrain had the opportunity to develop as a useful instrument of consciousness. Foetalization and retardation provide the opportunity for thinking.

Thinking as a Foetal Luxury

Man, homo sapiens, does not throw himself impulsively upon his prey, but has the capacity for restraint which is a function of his reflective organ. Many scholastic philosophers will shudder at the follies written by this philosophic outsider. The guns and tanks and planes, however, jump their prey and leave philosophy in rags. Today's world bears dramatic proof of thought as a reaction to the occurrences of the day. We get more and more "liberated" from the serene period of isolated scientific thinking which preceded the first World War. Today we are forced, nolens volens, to take a stand toward the events around us. It did not take Hitler long to convert many an idealistic philosopher into a spokesman for his madness.

Thinking as a Social Function

Thinking is a social instrument. We think and speak to someone, in relation to others. Thought is unconscious speech and communication. We must speak, even if only to the trees. Not until recently has the intellect become so aware of its social function of thought. It had remained aloof from wisdom and peace, power and wealth. Intelligence and technical thought were available for the highest bidder. They were at the service of drives and instincts, negligent of their social and harmonizing function. Thinking is a multifarious instrument with roots and stimuli in all organs, instincts and emotions.

Thinking is an attitude of the organism as a whole. Feeling and willing, striving and acting, cannot be differentiated from the reactive and reflective organism.

The psychologist has to try to unravel our complex split world of platonic fictitious thought and unguided animal action.

SECTION THREE

Adjustment by Retarded Reflection

Comparative psychology teaches us that the higher mammals still live in a world of pure sensations. Nevertheless, a primitive synthesis of sensations and new responsive actions does function, namely the so-called conglomerate of conditioned reflexes. The reflex, however, occurs without reflection, without the knowledge of knowing. This should immediately brake the action. Unlike lower animals, however, the mammal is able to adjust to a new environment. The insect is almost completely bound to its innate rigid instinctual actions. The insect remains chained to the reflexes brought about by the stimuli of the outside world. Only the highest mammal, the human being can synthesize the different sensations with his own observations and create the distinction between an inner world—the subject—and an outer world—the object. The insect can adjust only in the most limited way, that is, it can survive in a world already geared to its innate potentialities. The mammal, by means of the conditioned reflex, has the capacity for growing and changing adjustment. Man alone, with forethought, afterthought, self-reflection and self-observation at his disposal, can achieve an almost unlimited adjustment to his environment. His mind is an organ of adjustment. More effective than innate and conditioned reflexes, it teaches the organism to adjust itself to changed circumstances. The organism is free to select its form of adjustment. Consciousness of its aim determines the selection of stimuli. The instinct can adjust rapidly but is limited in scope. Thinking adjusts gradually but is unlimited.

Man is most adapted for adjustment to reality. Man, therefore, can also fear, anticipate and tolerate more than any other organism. Thinking is the retarding and tolerating process.

Via its sensations the animal is in continuous and direct communication with the outside world. *Man, however, opposes, confronts the outside world.*

Once reflection has been liberated from sensation and representation, it becomes pure and independent thinking. Thinking must be planned and be productive; it must be regulated and directed toward an adjustment and a real aim—thinking has to reflect something. Representations and feelings weaken thinking and regress it to the level of animal dependency on accidental impulses. Love makes us blind. Due to hormonal action people in love revert to magical thinking. The adult tackling of reality is supplanted by reflex actions springing from direct communication with a limited world.

On one hand, thinking widens the distance between man and his physical universe; on the other, it bends him toward it and sharpens his conception of reality. Thinking observes the personal struggle, observes the disentanglement of the biological chains and biological indispensabilities.

Thinking as a Function

Thinking is a developing function. Every thought process integrates previous and lower processes. Thinking is the function of growing consciousness and self-enlightenment. It is the instrument of readaptation. It is the ripening of prejudices into judgments. Man is never completely conscious but is always progressing toward complete consciousness, that is, toward a better adjusted approach to himself and reality. The growth of consciousness signifies the capacity of the organism to contemplate and confront reality.

Man gradually rouses himself from somnambulistic slumber to a waking contact with reality. Without difficulty, however, he slips back into sleepwalking and automatisms. Man can sleep with his eyes wide open without ever taking account of himself.

A few men become seeing prophets and show us a new reality. Most people, however, remain in a sleeping state having hardly opened their eyes. The thinking of others does not benefit us no matter how great its stature may be. Only our own readiness to think and verify for ourselves, to attack new problems benefits us. The ability of the thinker to put forth his thoughts demands the courage to doubt old truths and correct threadbare thoughts.

Thinking, as stated above, is coming to grips with reality. It is the probing and searching of reality with accepted propositions and the reshaping and reformulation of these where they no longer serve adequately. This coming to terms with reality takes place with an aim in mind, namely, the reshaping of reality. Interest and self-interest direct the thoughts, and thinking, however imperfect, is motivated movement toward a goal. This reshaping of reality takes place even under the most tragic circumstances. In concentration camps one of the first deeds was to rebuild the reality following some simple symbolic schemes, a womb, a house, some cozy corner; it was the only way to cope with the circumstances.

All psychological thinking implies identification with its object of study. It presupposes the feeling of oneness with the object of research. It feels itself a part of it. Because of its failure to grasp with care, psychology runs the risk of faulty observations. Its aims compel psychology to take this risk.

Since the thinking process implies memory and conscience, it requires the capacity for gathering and judging observed data. Thinking is the process of internal observation and selection of sensations, experiences, memories, judgments and evaluations to serve the purpose of a thought-aim. Von Monakow (19), the well-known Swiss neuropsychiatrist, referred in his book on hallucinations, to this judging, adopting and selecting instance as the beginning of moral conscience. Thinking aims at the stabilization of man grappling with reality. Without loving reality, we cannot cope with it. The original love we received from our environment made us accept its norms and value judgments, shaped our conscience (superego) and now demands an accounting for reality.

Thinking, then, consists of imaginative action and selection, a regulation of impressions and sensations with an aim in view. The psychologist refers to an intentional thinking "act", apart from all content of thoughts.

Thinking as an Ambivalent Function

Thinking, as much as speaking, is an ambivalent function. Thinking is the effort to acquire knowledge and is at the same time an intellectual play facilitating escape from the riddles of the world. Thinking is both a cognitive function and an active imaginative process which shapes a private, secluded world. It is simultaneous approach to and flight from reality, submission to nature and worship of idols.

Thinking and Feeling

The gradually expanding consciousness liberates itself slowly from the partly conscious, partly unconscious receptive world of feelings. Feeling is the partly conscious experiencing of emotions. Feeling is a reaction to the outer world directed by instincts. Every such reaction has components of pleasure and displeasure, depending on the impressions from without and drives from within. An impression without feeling does not exist; an impression without thinking does not exist. An impression is always partially an observation. Feeling and thinking are the inseparable function of becoming conscious.

Nevertheless, a continual polarity between thinking and feeling exists. I use my intelligence in certain instances and follow my feelings in others.

Thinking implies placing oneself in opposition to the world, yet acting with that world, conceiving that world. It implies choice, selection, arrangement, placement and active motion. Our impressions and reactions to the outside world and our relation to it are expressed in various terms of evaluations. Certain evaluations are directly dependent on the impact of the outside world. Scheler (17) referred to these as sense feelings, or reality feelings. Ego-feelings, or spiritual feelings, on the other hand, are much more dependent upon evaluations of the central selecting and judging instance, the thinking ego. Thinking becomes a function sufficient unto itself, apart and independent from reality, while feelings always maintain some relationship with this outside reality, however inappropriate they may be.

This latent dichotomy between feeling and thinking leads to erroneous assumptions. The human being needs the harmony of both a thinking and a feeling reality-response. The human being cannot permit over-evaluated affects to suffocate the intellect, or the biting intellect to kill the warm feeling. This is the explanation the psychologist provides for the split-personality prototype.

Thinking and feeling constantly alternate. Certain neurotic persons substitute thought for feeling. One cannot only think but must feel at the same time; man has to experience the world with all layers of his personality. In our period of civilization our feelings about many things are even more difficult to accept than our thoughts about them. Who, conscious of his moods, can accept and be happy with them? Fascism has taught us how destructive the solely emotional basis of thinking can be.

Thinking and Intellect

Consciousness grows out of observation, regulation, schematization, planning, abstraction—the polishing and chiseling of all these component functions to a thought-picture. There is a tendency to shape and fix such a picture instead of maintaining its mobility and vividness. Thinking actions tend to become rigid systems in the service of narrow aims. Man has a tendency to repeat his primary actions even when they are failures. The same phenomenon occurred with the unhappy laboratory dogs of Pavlov. The trained functional and useful reflex (conditioned reflex) became a useless automatism. Productive thinking is extension of the first thought and first deed to further suppositions and possibilities.

Intellect comprises not only the analytical research quality, but the vivid ability to search for a new aim and broaden the scope. The higher animals, too, act intelligently; that is, they adapt speedily to a new situation. Man, however, because of his eccentric position in the world, has special opportunities for developing his intellect. Vivid intellect, however, can regress to rigid automatisms and so resemble the innate instinct patterns. In man every automatism and rigid behavior pattern can revert again to a new adjustment. If this were not so, neurosis would be inaccessible to treatment.

Beyond the analytic, selective function, intellect is the vivacity and spiritual potency of life. Intellect becomes vulnerable when no personality is developed to fortify it. The cultural acquisition of intellectuals is easily paralyzed by terror and fear when character falters. Character, its potency, and the stable personality it provides for mental functioning is more important in society than a purely analytical intellect. This we could observe among the people who formed the resistance movement. The pure intelligentsia stayed away. In a full-grown personality feeling and thinking harmonize with each other.

The analytical part of the intellect, the selecting and sifting capacity, is forever hesitant. It opposes all that is accepted. It welcomes discussion and dialectic research. It breaks the spell of old thought concepts and paves the way for the spontaneous, creative function of the intellect. Unintelligence implies an inability to change, a rigid adherence to the same pattern, enslavement to habit.

Intellect can remain the sterile tool for selection and correction, the mere librarian of observed data. It can be creative only so long as it remains active, charged by the live personality.

Out of his delusions of greatness, man overestimated the technical intellect and neglected the instinctive, creative power that propelled it. The supertechnical surgeon, however, is helpless without the instinctual regenerative forces. Those forces heal the wounds inflicted by his tools. In every human being there dwells an instinctual unconscious technician operating outside the conscious functions. This formative intelligence, which makes or breaks us, can be studied by different methods beside the usual ones of psychoanalysis.

Pseudo-Intellect

We still tend to evaluate all labor of the mind as intellect instead of the thinking potency behind it. The human being comes into the world a bare, unprotected and unadapted animal, who can be subjected to various forms of training. He may even be made an imitative, mechanical thinking automaton. An intellectual is not necessarily a personality. On the one hand, training has created pedants, students, servile clerks—mental engineers who fall easy prey to the economically and mentally powerful. This form of imitative intellect is as much for sale as the labor of our hands and the power of our muscles. On the other hand scholarly training may make independent free thinkers of people who are forced to reorientate themselves as soon as they stand before a new situation. The real power of thinking is not imitation.

The over-development of technique and pseudo-intellect creates the myth that special training in a certain school or college produces more valuable personalities. The development of character and personality is subordinate to scholastic and technical achievement; to diplomas and report cards. The quiz can become a fatal instrument of education.

The last war taught us the danger inherent in the mass production of pseudo-intellectuals. They failed to resist overwhelming fatal emotions and capitulated to every outside mental power. Knowledge and philosophy were controlled by the blackjack. Many of the "intelligentsia", emotionally dissatisfied and disgruntled, surrendered to traitors and tyrants who ruled by intellectually-rationalized brutality.

Previous Theory of Delusions

Analysis reveals that instinct and affect, memory and conscience, are the roots of the thinking function. Love and hate penetrate our thinking and stimulate it to demonical activity. Gradually it becomes stripped of affects, but it cannot survive without feeling. Thinking loses its potency and contact when thoughts become isolated; one set point of view obscures all others. In our world too much is thought and not enough is felt. Thinking is stripped of its instinctual basis.

Delusion is a regression or isolation of the thinking function. It is either the dominance of archaic instinctual forms of thinking or the isolation of consciousness, the autonomy of thoughts without feelings. Delusion seeps gradually into the thinking function. It begins with a basis of truth, but the persistent error gradually supplants reality to such an extent that it is impervious.

Feeling must never be without thinking, thinking never without feeling. If either of these functions gains autonomy the individual loses his consciousness of and contact with reality.

Our science of thought has as yet failed to detach itself from the Aristotelian concept of *one* way of thinking. The science of physics was dominated by the same misconception until the period of the renaissance. It is regrettable that the experimental inquiry into thought processes is such a difficult procedure. (The Rorschach test has taught us a great deal about the relation between thinking and feeling and psychoanalysis has clarified the role of the unconscious.) I want this essay to be limited to the phenomenology of deluded thinking under normal circumstances. Delusions are incorrigible ideas for which many normal men are willing to die.

Delusion as Substitute

Let us first understand that delusion is inherent in normal thinking. The delusion treated by psychiatrists belongs to the same thinking process, but is fortified by pathological disturbances of the psychosomatic organism.

Thinking can be ruled by anarchy to such an extent that any formulation of ideas becomes impossible. The unconscious content of our thoughts may overwhelm our logical consciousness. The dream is the most normal example of this phenomenon of delusion.

In all growing processes of consciousness man reaches a limit. Beyond that limit thinking ends and faith begins: Credo quia absurdum. Delusion is a substitute belief. It is the enforcement of certainty instead of the acceptance of uncertainty. Delusion is the fear of uncertainty, of hesitation and skepticism. Just as the "idee fixe" defends the human being against the small vaccilations of life, the delusion defends us against the great leap into the obscure and unknown. Every acceptance of limits implies an obscure and unknown. Superstition is also a substitute for faith, it is a collective delusion, a remnant from previous magical and mythical conceptions of life. Delusion is the fear of realistic, critical thinking, the kind of thinking which is subject to criticism from without and the criticism from within that illuminates one's own subjective notions.

Hallucinations

The hallucination is a regression to a genetically older mode of feeling and observation in which ego and world are not yet distinct entities. This archaic orientation toward and contact with the outside world is dependent on functional disturbances of several organsystems. Otherwise it occurs only among children and primitive people. Since reality contact is disturbed, most of the hallucinations are the result of a chaotic projection of memory-pictures (engrams). (13)

When man is possessed by an overwhelming emotion, he immediately may hallucinate its possible causes. Fear produces hallucinations even more easily. The exhausted soldier on the battlefield envisions every automobile noise as an aerial attack of the enemy. Every social formation has its own collective illusions, hallucinations, revived images and primitive representations. These collective conceptions are never subject to discussion but only to blind acceptance. Every form of rite and suggestive training enforces these collective images. Many a member of such a collective can never be freed of such an unconscious, enforced image. In the delusion we become familiar with a similar process.

Thinking that Withdraws from Reality

Janet was one of the first to call the attention of psychology to the reality function (fonction du reelle). He speaks of a mental tension and force in man, the highest perfection of which is the reality-function. When this tension diminishes certain mental characteristics disappear. The first to weaken is the capacity for adjustment to changing reality. The immediate experience of, insight into and enjoyment of reality is a highly differentiated and vulnerable mental activity. Mature man, confronting reality, must have an alert adjustment.

"Carpe diem" is a vulnerable function. Most people's enjoyment is only the memory of experiences, the recounting of these to others. They are too exhausted to enjoy the supreme moment. They take snapshots of their experiences and relive them through the photograph album. "Kodakomania" is a form of mental ennui. But thinkers and dreamers, too, who withdraw into meditation are among those who cannot bear the tensions of reality. Escape into a system, or dogma relieves them of all tension. Their vague idealism bears an "as if" touch of reality. They withdraw into the abstraction, the isolated reality, the extraordinary.

Learnedness

Eventually we may prefer learnedness to wisdom. The learned and strange holds for us a magic fascination before which, like children, we bow. Learnedness grasps only that which has already developed and become rigid; it can never, however, follow the continuous stream of development. It is often a mixture of undeveloped wisdom and lust for power. The learned man is distracted and lacks contact with living reality. His system of thinking is a facade for inner doubt. His scientific display is often a well-regulated collection of plagiarisms.

It should now be easy to understand that conceit and partial delusion result from the loss of continuous, alert, and lively contact with reality. The study of these problems on a deeper level would reveal that these delusions and hallucinations, intensified, relate to the same mental disturbances. This essay, however, is concerned with the normal, rather than the pathological delusion.

Delusionary thinking can be called the continuation of primitive thinking without the correction by self-reflection. It is a withdrawal from reality. In all civilized thinking, however, these forms of thinking persist.

The Development of Thinking

To understand the above statement, we have to give up the dogma of identical thinking in all human minds. We may say that the more purified and technically trained thinking is, the more identical it becomes. Unconsciously the different laws of logic are accepted. The more primitive thinking is, the more confused feelings it contains and the less identical it is. It is possible, nevertheless, to study the general development of thought. It was analytical psychology which first called our attention to the gradually evolving relation to reality. The following stages in the development of a sense of reality may be distinguished (7).

First is the phase of intrauterine development, preceding birth, in which there can be little more than a feeling of satisfied omnipotence. There is no noxious outside world.

The stage of magic-hallucinatory potency follows birth. The child has the feeling of knowing and directing all. No distinction between an inner and outer world is drawn.

This phase is succeeded by initial attempts at conquest of the outside world with magic gestures. The child tries to command the world within his reach by pointing at it with his hands. Children feel that ideas are tangible and plastic. By keeping their lips stiffly closed they withhold evil thoughts. They also imbue inanimate objects with life. When they get hurt by bumping against a table, it is the table which beats them.

Out of this gestural thinking develops an uncritical animistic thinking, in which self-qualities are projected upon the outside world. All inanimate objects have a soul and no distinction between dead and alive is made. This thinking has a passive nature; thoughts are experienced as personified actions in which father, mother and siblings are the actors. Mythology is filled with such personifications. The adult, too, creates his personified delusions.

The following stage of magic thought is more active. It is a form of primitive strategy in which the spirits of objects are not only passively accepted but manipulated. The magic action attempts to seduce the spirits and to command them. The inner and outer world grow apart and magic thoughts are used to maintain contact between the two.

After the phase of imaginary omnipotence a change takes place. Unlimited power is granted not to the ego but to the outside world. In the games of children, every toy can become a symbol of parental power. Gradually this power and influence are incorporated and conscience is shaped by the penetration and incorporation of social values.

In these early stages of thinking the main influences emanate from the outer world. They overwhelm the thinking subject. His feeling of loss and helplessness is the same that we experience when we feel ourselves part of a mass. The regressed thinking of many psychotics reflects a similar experience; everything in the mind is experienced as an influence from outside. Archaic thinking is an almost wordless thinking, a kind of dream thinking and sinking away unto unconsciousness.

In totemistic thinking a symbolic displacement has already taken place. Good or bad spirits are represented or symbolized by a totem. In this projective thinking one's own power, misery and cruelty is transferred and attributed to the totem. The totem, the sacred animal, for instance, is the feared animal.

The confession to pure reality, the "adequatio cum re", the acknowledgment of preoccupation and prejudice of all wishing and thinking is the final phase of consciousness of reality. Nevertheless, it accepts responsibility for its limitations.

It takes some time before an independent judging ego is shaped, free from observations and images. The first ego is the product of observation rather than an independent entity. Primitive thinking is primarily affective thinking. The ego judges immediately under the influence of an observation and emotion. Only gradually this subjective form of thinking adjusts itself to reality. In adult thinking the archaic illusion of almighty power may lead to self-overestimation and egocentricity.

The evolution of individual thinking is paralleled in the growth of civilization.

Archaic or Primitive Thinking

During the last few decades primitive thinking has been subjected to careful study. This is due not only to progress in the fields of ethnology and anthropology, but also to the realization that analogous forms of thinking could be found in children, psychotics and the unconscious of every human mind. The idea has also developed that the difference between civilized and primitive thinking is one of degree. Many present primitive societies are the descendants of formerly civilized peoples.

Primitive thought is not less logical than mature thought. Sensual experiences, however, are less adequately controlled and the reaction is a far more emotional one. The primitive confronts the world with more affectivity. He lives in a world of continually existing fear toward which he is constantly alerted. Constant tension prevails between himself and his environment. His feelings are more explosive, his actions more instinctive. Modern man of the Atomic Age shares the same attitudes to some extent.

The European of the Middle Ages was still a man of uncontrolled emotionality. His actions were affect-ruled. The mourner was paralyzed by sorrow for weeks; the sad man displayed his feelings with theatrical complaints. Collective hallucinations and delusions were experienced with greater ease (20). Collective myths, alive in all, came to the fore more easily.

Primitive thinking is not subject to argumentation and correction and is almost insensitive to experience. If it fails to coincide with the reality situation, its errors are ascribed to mysterious influences from without. The primitive easily resorts to pretexts and magic forces to explain his failure. Hidden qualities take precedence over actual ones.

The primitive rejects logic. B may be equal to A or not, depending on the wishes of strange powers. The archaic thinking is concept- and habit-bound. It is dominated by the images and emotions of the collectivity, which easily abandons logic. Its own rules are elementary and infinite in power.

The archaic psyche has an unlimited memory. It is comparable to our own subconscious. The primitive man is familiar with a large quantity of images and words. His language, usually more complex than our own, does not combine word pictures to form abstractions. What he thinks he sees, he sees. That is why he lives in a hallucinated world. Affect and drive rule his observations. A vague feeling, a superficial resemblance, an insignificant totem carry more meaning than generalized concepts. Man, animal and inanimate object bear mystical relationships to each other. The world is colored with subjective expectation and the expectations are hallucinated. Primitive conception of life supposes a "mystic participation" existing between man, animal and inanimate object.

When the primitive comes into contact with an ominous totem, he may die of fear. In his pre-logical form of thinking no distinction between conscious and unconscious is made. Primitives dream aloud, so to speak. The fearful dream becomes reality; unpleasant reality is fantasied away. In Northern Borneo, all dreams are interpreted as real. The man who dreams that his wife is unfaithful to him has the right to disown her.

Identifying or Magic Thinking

In primitive societies a man does not live far apart from his fellows. A relationship of common fate and mutual thought pervades primitive community life. The thoughts of one member of the tribe, for instance, can endanger the entire community. The word as such has suggestive and destructive power. The victor who slays an enemy is imbued with the power of the dead man. The Dajaks in Borneo believed that the decapitation of their enemies would fortify them with the power of the killed. One is what one possesses.

The artistic remnants of pre-historical man are interpreted as examples of magic thinking. The pre-historic hunter inscribed his prey on a rock wall so as to gather greater power. Creative art was a magic action performed as a symbolic conquest of future prey. Our unconscious is still permeated with magic archaic power. The twentieth century slave is too dependent on his technical intellect to show concern for his magic, yet a Teutonic magician restored him to a stage of collective madness. The economic logic of our time has rejected all magic and fears the untouchable possibilities of long forgotten worlds. It does not dare to live side by side with the shadows of long ago.

Yet all objective knowledge preserves the magic experience of unity. Every higher form of thinking embodies earlier forms.

Participating Thinking

There are many causes for regression to primitive thinking. Terror and persecution, slavery and famine can reverse high civilization to more primitive modes of mentality. Recall the extinct Negro civilizations of central Africa, the civilizations of the Mayas and Aztecs. Even more clearcut are the many examples of primitive thinking we find in our own present-day society.

We call participating thinking (mystic participation) (12) that form of identificatory thinking that accepts no difference between inner thought and physical occurrence. This form of thinking assumes that inner thoughts precipitate a change in our fellow beings and even in inanimate objects. Every thought wields influence. Our prayers are reminiscent of that type of thinking. Thinking implies active participation in collective events. Barriers between individuals are non-existent, and each individual participates in the thinking of the entire world.

Growing consciousness, however, opposes reality as critical judge and observer. The public in the theater considers itself a participant in the dramatic action.

Participation Through Isolation of Culture

Participating thinking spreads if the community remains isolated. We shall see how this may cause mass delusions in a modern civilization.

In a closed circle of conversation some magic participating thinking occurs.

The same type of thinking goes on within a school or university. Students preserve the thinking of their school years. Even the scholar experiences difficulty in liberating himself from the suggestion of his philosophical instructor.

Participating-thinking imbues life with all kinds of rites. Without these, the world would not be what it is. We experience this clearly with the thinking of the Malayan people among whom a general feeling of spiritual participation prevails. Everyone is invested with a soul, whether dead or alive. Everything is imbued with good or evil forces. The man who covers his dagger with saliva thus makes it part of himself and assures his own immunity. In Java people open doors and chests to facilitate the birth of a child. The world is a magic helper in everything that affects the individual. Similar concepts survive in popular medical superstition. The weak child is made to eat horse-meat and drink ox-blood. The father partakes of the medicine when his child is ill. The newborn infant is protected from future trouble by burial of the placenta and so forth.

In the periphery of our consciousness participating thinking lives on. The most acutely critical person experiences moments of vague and relaxed meditation in which archaic forms of thinking come to the fore together with day dreams and half-dreams in which no differentiation between object and subject is made. In sleeping and dreaming the archaic world takes complete possession of us.

Mythical Thinking

Man likes to live in myth. He converts his fatherland into a legend, a beautiful fairy tale. He speaks of the old European liberalism and the new American democracy while he by-passes reality with all its subtleties.

As part of a mass, as members of a crowd, our identifications and participations come to the fore with greater ease. The meeting of a former schoolmate immediately precipitates patterns of former student-thinking; adolescent thoughts are reactivated, we relive the beautiful myth of our youth.

Identification in Thinking

As the native identifies with the totem in his group, so do more civilized groups identify with their subtly concealed totems. If our home town is subjected to criticism we spring to its defense. We identify with our school, our town, our country. At a meeting in which this topic of disguised identification was discussed a philosopher debated rather indignantly: "My Groningen-heart is revolted." In his criticism he had identified with the theories of his university. We identify with our countries, our climates, our class, with the layer of the population to which we belong and with its way of thinking. We identify especially with our possessions. The more we possess, the more difficult it becomes for us to renounce either the possessions as such or the theories which justify our having them.

Certain remnants of archaic thinking permeate our daily existence. Take, for instance, "lese majeste". It is a rather primitive conception that damage to the name or damage to the picture implies damage to the person himself. The magic man lives on within us.

A preconceived idea, a rooted, fixed way of thinking is often such a remnant. It is as if archaic thinking continued to contaminate our well-adjusted system of thought.

There exists a refined form of identifying thinking. To empathize or sympathize with another is impossible without this thought process. The serious psychologist has to utilize this process to familiarize himself with his fellow human beings. Psychology, therefore, maintains certain aspects of a magic science. Such thinking processes, however, are of slight value to the physical scientists.

False Figurative Language

Since our daily language so frequently resorts to allegory and figurative speech, we can assume that man feels a tremendous need for identification. Whenever we are anxious to prove something, we refer to an analogous case. These analogies, which play on feeling rather than logic, are dangerous for our thinking. A political speech, for instance, can overwhelm and narcotize by a flood of suggestive pictures and allegories. When our feelings are aroused we lose our critical ability and insight and reactivate earlier, incorrect concepts of reality. False figurative language dims our thinking.

The Dictatorship of Imagery

In primitive thinking as well as in our trained twentieth century mind imagery plays an almost dictatorial role. Ask a philosopher to walk the plank over an abyss—as Pascal proposed—and he will hesitate as much as the child who has no reason. The imagined risk defies all logic.

Images and representations exert a formative influence on our organism; they are creative thoughts. Wrong and good images act deeply on our biological being and produce organic reactions. The science of hypnosis teaches us these facts.

Contemporary life overwhelms the human brain with the most chaotic impressions and images. Propaganda and advertisement, the manifold forms of distractions create such chaos of impressions that logic can no longer find its way. Man has become hypersensitive to suggestion. We are grateful to anyone who takes us in hand and clears our path through the chaos of our thoughts and images.

Wishful Thinking

The subjective wish as well directs our thinking. Our daydreams and undefined wishes are forever misinterpreting reality. There is chaos in our thinking. Sorrow and defeat and all other emotions are continuously playing on the direction of our thoughts. Pride and bitterness revolve our thoughts in an eternal vicious circle.

Totalitarian Thinking

Totalitarian or dictatorial thinking is a remnant of archaic times. Objective verification of ideas is rejected since no reality beyond the dictatorial opinion exists. The deviant point of view is considered dangerous for the weak. Free thought is experienced as a thwarting, hostile force. The critical word, the deviating attitude, the non-conformism of one man threatens the clan. The individual is only permitted to think with the tribe. Archaic thinking follows what we might call an imperialistic strategy. It lulls people to sleep, it resists their consciousness and critical confrontation, it suppresses all individual creativity. Totalitarian thinking is identifying thinking; it takes account only of totalities and never of parts. Specific and particular forms have no value. Only the recurrent and expected is accepted. Man remains one with his people, his land, his race. Human evolution, however, breaks the bond between man and his world and places him in opposition to it.

In time of war primitive attitudes come to the fore in all fighters. The individual is only part of an organism. The army is hypersensitive to criticism. There is no sense of humor—the army offends easily. Blood revenge and collective punishments are again made use of. Collectivities are held responsible for the deeds of individuals.

In the highly vulnerable feeling of military honor one finds much archaic thinking. To lose face, to be shamed, is equivalent to a beating. The aggressive word demands revenge as much as the bullet. Restrictions placed on the topics of discussion by soldiers and enemy aliens are a further reflection of the authoritarian attitude.

Primitive civilizations are more keenly aware of the need for respect of leaders and superiors. In Java, for example, a respectful language, devoid of the aggressive and sharp words of everyday speech, is used in addressing superiors. In occupied Europe a great many had to learn restraint in their speech. Expression of individual thinking was severely punished by the magic Teuton.

Traditional Thinking

We find the archaic way of thinking in all forms of traditional thought, rooted in fixed patterns of feeling, acting and thinking. Tradition is the continuum of mass action. School already forces ideas into the harness of dogma. Only after intense conflict is the personality able to free itself from this tradition.

It is one of the paradoxical tasks of teaching to form fixed patterns of thinking in the student. The learning man must first embrace that which is handed down from the past. Beyond this, however, he must be taught to confront and criticize what he has learned. The true school prepares its students for free thinking—thinking that is capable of renewing and correcting itself continuously. "La tradition, c'est la democratie des morts."

SECTION FIVE

Thought and Language

Thought and language are intimately related to each other. All memory of mankind, all tradition, are enclosed in language. Language reveals old historical traditions. He who creates new words opens up new territories of thought.

The word raises man above the level of the animal. It provides the opportunity for mental contact. Gesture and mimicry are the oldest forms of communication. Indians and Greeks made use of a sign language, and remnants of sign language are still found in the Javanese dances. But we too use gesture and mimicry subconsciously. At times we use a theatrical gesture to make ourselves understood, and a wink, a hidden laugh, a cough, can change the meaning of an earnest word.

In a later phase of development sound and speech become our chief means of communication. Timbre, velocity of expression and gesture as well, constantly change the meaning of words.

Primitive languages express sensual variations and concrete peculiarities with a tremendous richness of distinction. They are unfamiliar with the symbolic condensations, displacement and transference of meanings, which, for instance, the mathematical sciences use. Hence, primitive man must resort to manifold distinctions. He cannot arrive at a general insight—his language affords no opportunity for thinking in generalizations. He speaks in a pictorial way, as the poet, he identifies in word and gesture with the expressed situation.

Language—the gradually expanding treasury of words—is always the expression of a special kind of thinking. That is why language may block our attempt to attain a purer and better form of thinking. Gradually, customary language becomes too limited for special ways of thinking. This is why thoughts must continually strive to free themselves from the existing language and must create new word symbols in order to express new and better thoughts. With our mother's milk we swallow a special language and with that language, anchored habits of thought.

The Language of the Child

The first verbal expression of the child is usually a monosyllabic prattling, much like that of animals, used to indicate the aim of his drives. Natural sounds are imitated. The dog is "wuf, wuf", the cat "meow, meow", etc. Soon the sounds and half-words are utilized as magic strategy. When the baby says "fair", he means chair, give me that chair, I want to do something with that chair. The child endows the object with life through the use of the word.

When babies converse in their broken tongue they do not ask for a logical compromise. They talk with no thought of relating the different parts of their conversation. The same abracadabra recurs in the language of senile patients.

The word which was originally attached to the object and considered an integral part of it, later becomes endowed with an independent existence of its own. The child begins to grasp that the word is a creation of human intelligence. The more keenly he senses that the word belongs to him, the more the child is able to free himself of his inner fixation to the rest of the physical world.

As we have already seen, identification with and feeling for someone are the incipient processes of reality contact. Without these "human" qualities, deeper communication between beings is impossible. However, by naming things, the child partially frees himself of this process of identification and acquires the notion of a real world distinct from the "I". The monosyllabic nominative thinking of the child is the beginning of his capacity for confronting reality.

Word and Intonation

Our word is a manifold being. Every word evokes visual images from our unconscious. We first thought in pictures, later in words. In dreams we revert largely to the world of pictures.

The pronunciation of words as such changes their meaning. Every word has its significance but at the same time its unconscious background. Words are expression, but also disguise. They are a living act with peripheral scenes and hidden motives.

Sound-Languages

Sound and rhythm often have a more important function than the specific meaning of the word. Eros especially colors ordinary words and makes them deep and significant. Would it even be possible to write the semantics of the half-words and sounds that people in love use as a means of conversation? The murmuring and small names between mother and baby mean words of love indescribable in stark definitions.

There are languages which rely more than others on undefined emotional sounds. German words often have more sound than real meaning. Appealing more to mass and sentiment than reason, they keep the words caught in ambivalence, suspended between emotion and intellect. It was a strange experience to hear the vocal disguise of Goebbels propaganda thrown over one during the Nazi-occupation.

Word-Magic

Words may become magic symbols, condensations of meanings endowed with special power. This is seen especially in the rapt, repetitious phrases of the child. The expression of the word signifies the attainment of power over the indicated object. Words themselves become powerful.

During the evolutionary phase of a word especially, during its period of detachment from an object, the value of the word and its power become especially great. The words become bold flashes of lightning with which one can banish, beat or praise. How many snobs there are, whose loaded words tyrannized their surroundings! With a master-word, one can conquer masses.

The magical quality of the word is greater than most of us realize. How many of us "touch wood" when we express a certain word? We fear that the word with its magic background attracts danger.

This superstitious influence is especially pronounced in vague, undefined words. Their contact with the unconscious is closer and they therefore exercise more power. To move the masses one has to make use of such vague terms whose real significance defies definition. The therapist uses the magic influence of the word when asking the patient to express freely his feelings. The verbalization of vague feelings is of great cathartic value.

The Power of Talk

Endless talk my conquer fear. One fears silence. Those who least understand the world in which they live are its most talkative citizens.

Propaganda tries to achieve its aim through endless repetition and the constant dinning in of words. The masses like mythical words and the sledgehammer blows of windy speeches. Clear expression becomes heresy. The word that evokes the most bizarre associations becomes the most beloved. Everyone projects his own unfulfilled wishes upon it.

The preachers of penitence in the Middle Ages were familiar with the suggestive power of words. Their word-pictures of hell could transport whole masses into a state of religious ecstasy. In our age the loudspeaker has assumed that task.

People are possessed with a motoric lust for talk. Many dogmas and political theories appeal to this motoric lust-pattern. They gratify a universal need for talk which abreacts vague fears rather than promoting a real understanding of their message.

Crypto-Archaisms

It is difficult to free our thinking from hidden archaisms. After the first world war, many crypto-archaisms came again to the fore. There was a preference for the emotional and the ecstatic, the elementary and the chaotic. In the field of art, futurism and dadaism were the fads of the day. This rebellion against civilized refinements was rationalized with theoretical explanations of the respect for the primitive. Jazz was preferred to more traditional musical forms, expressionism replaced naturalism.

One could also find these crypto-archaisms in the lability and suggestibility of human opinions. Year after year new dogmas were presented to an eager audience. The extreme was defended. Romantic attitudes toward crime and gangsterism developed and the criminal was idealized. The intelligentsia, especially, provided fertile ground for this peculiar fluctuating thinking. They did not know what to confess or what to believe and bent to each passing wind. In central Europe the adoration of the people's mentality (das Volkische) was a triumph of archaic thinking.

In retrospect, such crystal-clear dogmas and proven theories are later seen to belong to a certain period. Even for the man of science, the more objective he considers himself, the less aware he is of the subjective premises of his knowledge.

SECTION SIX

Causal and Final Thinking

The causally-oriented theoretician tries to reduce reality to generally valid rules. The smaller probability becomes absorbed into a larger probability. He is not taken up with the accidental constellation of reality, but only with the manifest causal chain. Causes and consequences were at work in the world, even when they remained unobserved by the thinking individual. It is impossible for us to view something outside these causal relations. We are confronted everywhere with the outcomes of causes. Causality dissects the continuum of reality into a series of sections. It responds to the human preference for regularity, for interrelated and dependent facts, for continual and gradual development. It does so, even where reality does not correspond. Final thinking, however, tries to discover the sense and significance of historical events. Every historical event is an accidental "cross-section" of continuity. The individual conceives of the "accidental happening", the "unique event" (Einmaligkeit) only as a phase of historical, purposeful reality. Indeed, creative thinking tries to free itself of archaic automatisms and aims at planning before acting. This tendency to plan, to develop a thought-program, is projected by man onto external affairs. For him there is no accident. Historical events are symbolic meeting-places of the historical process and the historical cause. Reality never changes suddenly; the foundations for these changes are laid underground and come to the fore as historical facts. From the causal point of view, occurrences are living proof of prevailing laws. From the final point of view, the concrete event is an incidental happening in the service of a greater aim. Both forms of thinking aim to create eternal continuity out of the chaotic present.

Laws of Thinking

Thanks to the influence of Aristotle, philosophy is burdened with formal laws of thinking. Aristotle's postulate of the identity of thinking is an incorrect one. Even philosophers in their discussions don't think in the same way. Their education, training, social environment and other factors combine to determine their way of thinking. Acquaintance with other systems of thought invalidates Aristotelian logic. The Brahman philosophy, for instance, preaches that human sorrow begins with thinking, that thinking is revolt against the Gods and bans us from the truth.

Aristotle's principle, nevertheless, provided the thinkers of twenty centuries with a meeting ground and formalized laws of thought. Other civilizations demonstrate that common modes of thinking are the product of a culture.

The imperialistic European thinker, of course, considered other systems of thought as primitive and less refined. Participating thinking, magic thinking were attributed only to natives. Gradually, however, the realization grew that our forms of thinking were permeated with these forms of thought. The idealistic German system, for instance, surrendered without protest to the participating Nazi philosophy.

Western and Eastern Thinking

Western thinking is restless. The Western spirit is impelled toward activity. The Eastern thinker does not think with the same motility. He enjoys a static state, rest and contemplation. He is more open to inner visions than to illusions of the senses based on external stimuli. Western thinking is geared toward the broadening of its views of the world. Eastern thinking does not search for disparate point of views. It does not define but creates inner worlds.

Western civilization makes use of confronting thinking. Its logic-loving mentality places itself in opposition to rather than in the midst of reality. It belongs essentially to an individuating civilization. The

Aristotelian logic belongs to him who, in his loneliness, touches the world with critical antennae. This touching has an element of danger, since it may alter reality. There is always a destructive element in restless touching and tasting of the world. Nervous, obsessional thinking and verifying continually destroys part of its own world-picture.

Once the individualistic man conforms to the logical laws of thinking, all other forms of thinking become illogical or primitive to him. He praises only what is adequate in terms of his own system. Logic, however, also embraces a series of rules which are made use of as long as they prove adequate. Who can tell what other means of gaining consciousness remain unexplored (metaphysical, parapsychological) as a result of the dictatorship of Aristotelian thinking? The clinician knows that the exploration of the apparently chaotic unconscious yields a treasure of knowledge about man and universe.

European logic, however, nearly always fails in actual life. It is difficult to convince people in a logical way; they are eager to convict and mistrust logic. They justify their actions in terms rooted in unconscious wishes and drives. Logic remains only one means for cataloging reality.

Types of Consciousness

Psychology has tried to classify the ways of gaining consciousness of oneself and the world. The roads toward reality are manifold. The typical separation is dependent on the means chosen toward gaining consciousness of the world. Jung (10) and Van der Hoop (21) distinguish intuitive types, feeling types and thinking types. Although any such classification is rather artificial, it offers insight into the varied character structures of man, and his reasons for choosing a particular road toward reality.

Male and Female Thinking

Let us take an example of different approaches to reality. In reality there is no pure distinction between masculine and feminine thinking; both forms exist in everyone in varying degree.

Man is more of a specialist, concerned with specific aspects of the universe. He is one-sided, and stronger because of this one-sidedness. Woman is more of a generalizer. Her functions demand familiarity with many things that man treats with disdain. She must know a little of a great many things while the man seeks to know a great deal about few. Ancient science went through a generalizing feminine approach.

Modern science has passed through a male stage of research, namely a specialistic stage. Until a few decades ago only the male was permitted to study science. That is why modern science bears the aspect of male aggressive power. Those who restrict themselves to highly specialized knowledge have the opportunity to attain power. This power is part of the Western ideal.

Male thinking is one-sided and split thinking. Particularly pronounced in the male is the split between thinking and feeling to the extent that he is unable to relate the two.

In the future, science must become more conscious of the new need for generalized integrated knowledge. It will have to become more female in character. Female thinking is more realistic; it is imbued with more sense and feeling for practical adjustment.

The woman with deep and clear intellect, who yearns for creative expression in science, remains, however, burdened throughout her life with the care of her children and family. After maturing considerably, she becomes aware that she has gathered through her multifarious experiences wisdom not learned and abstract, but real and warm and full of life.

Anatomical Thinking

The sharp, dissecting thinking, which destroys feelings, is unaware of moral value judgments. It makes no distinction between good and evil.

Anatomical thinking—due to its lust for pure dissection—is heartless. It is aware only of objective morphological relations, not of human beings. It is incapable of penetrating the mysteries of man. It lacks the capacity for identification and intuition. It cannot identify with the world into which it probes. It cannot rid itself of the idol of mirror-like objectivity. Complete knowing is impossible, however, without loving.

Anatomical thinking became a means of gaining power. He who could handle it well could subject the world and his fellow beings. This is the main reason for the worship of cold, intellectual thinking and critical dissection.

Such thinking, however, may cause neurosis and unhappiness in its students. It creates a bulwark of intellect against feeling and emotion. Such people no longer live, but only read and think about life. The world is reduced to a cold and loveless existence, a formula without inner sense.

Biological Roots of Thinking

All thinking has biological roots. Thinking requires certain foods and fluids for growth, a special diet and special physical exercise. Certain rites and rhythms alter thinking. The gastronomist thinks in another way than the aesthete who tries to purify his thought by fasting.

We witness the arousal of self-awareness in those who are successful erotic partners and its disappearance among those whose sexual pride was hurt. Woman nearly always places her thinking in the service of an erotic aim. Male thinking derives more satisfaction from maintaining a logical equilibrium.

All ideas demand a vital basis. They get lost in a vacuum without it.

Shallow Modes of Thought

Many thinkers live among big and idle thoughts and words, borrowed from books, rather than derived from experience. Unaware of life's reality, they think in the same way in which the child plays with colorful soap-bubbles, watching the brilliance and color of the bubble until it bursts.

It is the infantile philosopher in us who is seduced by weighty thoughts and impressive plans. But we use this play as training for the realities of life. We learn to select from superfluous wisdom.

In practical life we are able to distinguish other forms of thinking, dependent on the special adjustment of the individual. We distinguish dogmatic thinking, wishful thinking, labeling thinking, juridical thinking, political thinking, modish thinking. All these speak for themselves.

Labeling Thinking

Only two forms of thinking, dangerous to everyday practice, are mentioned here. Labeling thinking is that which attaches labels to all thinking human beings. If one once belonged to a certain school, class, or race one's opinions and language are forever regarded as part of this school, class, or race. Once labeled, the label can never be lost. Forever, we have to belong to a certain rubric. What lives behind the label doesn't matter.

Juridical Thinking

Juridical thinking is another rigid form of interpreting life and its habits. Because men require rules and laws for the limitation of each other's instincts, the man of law seeks to reduce all spontaneous life to similar rules and laws. He thinks in a codified world and views people as its codified inhabitants. It was this form of anti-psychological thinking which ruled international relations between the two world wars. The United Nations are still in danger of viewing peace as a purely codified Valhallah.

SECTION SEVEN

Normal Delusions

Francis Bacon (2) in his Novum Organum was the first to view delusions of the spirit and errors of thinking from a psychological standpoint. He rejected all rigid philosophical abstractions. Because of its rigidity theory can become the wrong object of thinking rather than reality. Bacon reproached his predecessors for living too much in theory and not enough in reality. Our thoughts are representatives of ourselves, rather than of reality.

Theory aims at subjecting reality to its own dictatorship. Human intellect is no pure instrument of research but is bound to influences of feeling and will; what man would like to see as true, he believes as true. Hence, Bacon advises us to approach with suspicion all that which the spirit accepts greedily. Fantasy is the greatest enemy of the intellect. This conceit of thought Bacon refers to as general delusion, the "idola generis".

He calls special delusion, "idola specus", that type of human thought which is colored by man's special characteristics, by his temperament, his mood, his yearning.

Language, the unstable vehicle of thought, also leads to delusion and error. Don't the phrases and definitions of philosophers serve to disguise their nude irresolution? Bacon calls this delusion of words and labels "idola theatri". Catchword and label accomplish their greatest triumph in establishing a mass-delusion. The famous English statesman and philosopher was referring especially to the dogmas and theatrical parading of philosophers which only served to justify the creations of their own imagination. They were thought-plays detached from reality and representative only of the mind of their conceited creator. A person's cherished dogmas reveal his personality. The manifold systems of philosophers describe more adequately the philosophers themselves than the world of realities, according to Bacon. Can we add anything better to this concept of delusion and conceit? Bacon's ideas are as valid today as they were three centuries ago.

Seductive Stupidity

When intellect can no longer contribute to the knowledge of the world, when our spirit is no longer potent enough to struggle with the facts of the day, we take recourse to the stupidity and "innocence of childhood".

We experienced this regressive behavior and escape from consciousness most pointedly during the years of occupation and terror, and understood it as a natural defense against pain and sorrow. But there is another more seductive way of flirting with superficiality and playing with stupidity. There is a yearning to return to the land of morons. We are relaxed and gay when we hear the radio voices carry us back to a realm which does not require our brain. Gradually we become more and more infected with silliness and escapism. Why should we think? Why should we fight to understand this world? Why not remain in comfortable stupidity?

Superfluous Thinking

Thinking often has a firmer grasp on some of us than we expect. Thoughts often remain rooted in our mind; we are possessed with a problem and we cannot escape its answer and the consequent presentation of newly aroused problems. We would prefer to idle away and yet a cogitating fury lives in us. We destroy things by thinking and destroy ourselves with it in the delusion that only thinking solves our problems. The self-temptation of superfluous thought and the restless overestimation of our own brain makes us suspicious. This is reminiscent of the baby's strategy. The repetition of the same gruesome tale helps him to conquer his vague, bigger fear. Similarly the adult tries to free himself from "the great fear of being in the world" by compulsively torturing his own brain.

Obsessional Thinking

This form of obsessional thinking exercises a narcotic influence. Gradually unconscious drives take possession of our thought. Thoughts arise which cannot be mastered. They are feared and alien to us, yet we cannot rid ourselves of them. They are absurd yet they possess us. There is a tragic relation between cogitating, ruminating and meditating. Vague thoughts may become rooted in our mind as symbols of suppressed unconscious drives.

The Autonomy of Ideas

Every thought as such has a growth-potential. It can expand to an all-embracing image that suppresses all other ideas. He who creates ideas may become possessed by them. The idea may become detached from him, subdue all other ideas and precipitate unwilled actions. In reality every new thought leaves its creator and lives its own life. It may stimulate the imagination of other people. Dostoiewski describes Raskolnikov as one who was dragged away by one pure idea. Fascinated by an isolated thought the hero justifies the crime in the service of his lust for power.

It is as if in every idea some mystic archaic powers remained alive. With one simple idea, with one catchword, one can sow poison and hate as well as blessings for many people. Think, for instance, of the treatment by Coué, who tried to heal neurotics by the monotonous repetition of one simple idea and image. All these phenomena can occur because thinking is a biological function, comparable to other motor and sensory functions. Every thought is an unconscious action.

The Delusion of Certainty

Only the reflexive animal is instinctively certain. Man is and remains unsteady in his thinking. His world is neither ready, nor fixed, nor limited, but must grow. From one uncertainty he must move on to others. The nineteenth century was too much preoccupied with constant norms and evaluations and too insensitive to the dynamics of its own system of thought.

He who firmly asserts his certainty is often surpressing his doubt and evading the vacuum of his ignorance. Every delusion is endowed with the same inner certainty we find in primitive thinking. It does not create problems. Delusion is a regression, a theatrical disguise of inner impotence. This process does not refer to pathology only. It occurs in everyday thinking.

The scientists of the last century were possessed by the delusion of hasty declaration and explanation. Many theories preceded the facts. Many scientists wrote off as understandable and transparent that which remained secret and obscure. By atomization of the infinite they tried to profane unsolved mysteries.

Thinking is the equalization of chaos, the reduction of single accidental occurrences to generalized happenings. Every theoretical reduction, however, omits the secret of the unique historical accident, the mystery of the individual event.

Man overestimates his instinctual certainties. Thinking extinguishes the certainty of innate knowledge. Recall the story of the thousand-footed insect who was interrogated by the cunning fox. From the day he was asked which foot he set in motion first, he could no longer walk; he was paralyzed by the new problem. Instinctual certainties disappear as soon as they reach the domain of reflection and thought. Feeling alone can give certainty. Thinking and reflection create doubt. That is why art provides straighter insight into truth than philosophy.

It is the tragedy of man that thought has brought him to new uncertainties. He has partaken of the tree of knowledge and is expelled from the paradise of instinctual life. This does not mean, however, that his thinking is always striving toward reason and logic. Rationalism and irrationalism, mature and archaic thinking develop side by side.

Proverbial and Patterned Thinking

Most thinking processes take place outside our consciousness. It is thinking in usual patterns. These patterns are lifted from popular wisdom, proverbs and the manifold crystallizations of collective knowledge. The proverb, above all, is suggestive of a philosophy of acquiescence. Collective knowledge continuously builds and stimulates our individual thinking. In all our arguments we must fight against inadmissible generalizations. Popular psychology embraces those generalizations. Mass knowledge is inert.

The patterning of thought is enhanced by the industrialization and standardization of life. Our brain is a maze of fixed patterns, slogans and clichés. It has become a bad camera for recording reality.

Through continuous facing of reality man must conquer it gradually. In youth he learns to see reality through special colored glasses, in special patterns. Gradually, however, he must change those patterns and relate them to reality. It is as if through the growing process of thinking a kind of reality organ develops in man.

The Subject Thinks

In all thought concerned with reality, the thinking and creating subject remains the greatest riddle to himself. The self, the ego, the focal point of every world view, remains its own greatest source of confusion. Every world picture is a subjective creation, no matter how minutely the subject thinks he has copied the world. The most objective copy still contains a subjective view. The graphologist will tell us that every handwriting, originally a fixed pattern of letters, is different. Children, in copying the simplest pictures, distort them in accordance with their own character.

How varied our subjective thinking is! Some overflow with original ideas, while others remain content with simple imitations.

The Unconscious as Creator of Our Thinking

Why do subjects think so differently? For the psychoanalyst the answer is not difficult. In every hour with his patients, he is aware not especially of his patient's thinking but of his confused reactions to unconsciously formed ideas. Thinking is the constant struggle against the preconceived patterns of our mind. The unconscious guides the willing conscious mind, which accepts, justifies or rationalizes the deeper notions.

Men's thoughts are propelled by the creative forces of their unconscious. Through special technique the ego can grow aware of these unconscious motives. Our desire for clarity, our fight to gain new insights gives us a partial conception of structural relations. The deepest levels, however, remain hidden.

The unconscious sees with a philosophical eye. The conscious justifies the limitations of its own understanding. What is new insight? It is a sudden release of tension. The unconscious suddenly clarifies our mind and we can either defy or acknowledge it. The road we choose depends on the degree of our self-knowledge.

Fashionable Thinking

There is a fashion of ideas and arguments similar to that of hats and dresses. Out of tradition one can incorporate certain fashionable ideas. Man is possessed by more lust for imitation and tradition than for creation of original ideas. It is as if several instincts clashed in the process of thinking. There is a social instinct which induces imitation and identification. Simultaneously there is an individualistic instinct which demands distinction and the formulation of a personal vision as opposed to that of collectivity.

Some ideas have a pandemic character and work like an infectious agent the individual is unable to resist. The idea finds such deep resonance that man is dragged away by it. Forty years ago the word "socialist" was applied as a nickname to people. Today, socialism is an ideal for those who not long ago spoke of it disapprovingly. In our time, "communism" is the catchword for all that is taboo.

Scapegoating

Scapegoating grows out of normal attitudes, normal biases and ordinary prejudices. Its most famous example is found in the rituals of the Hebrews and is depicted in the Book of Leviticus. On the Day of Atonement, a live goat was chosen. The high priest, attired in linen garments, laid both hands on the goat's head and confessed over it the iniquities of the children of Israel. The sins of the people having thus been symbolically transferred onto the beast, it was taken out into the wilderness and let loose. The people felt purged, and for the time being, guiltless. (1).

The tendency to revert to this primitive level of thinking has persisted. People are forever seeking scapegoats, most often in human form, whom they can saddle with their misfortunes and misdeeds. "Civilized people" remain primitive in their thinking.

Such events have occurred throughout history. The victims have always been small minority groups who, because of conspicuousness and tradition, became the bearers of the burden of blame.

Nominative Thinking

In his thinking the simple man is fixated to names. By naming things he feels that he has explained them. Primitive languages are characterized by vast numbers of names and words with fine nuances of meaning. The king of the Middle Ages was surrounded by innumerable pages, lackeys, grooms, etc. Every royal function called for another servant with another name. Every function was named. The same happens in the mind; all that remains incomprehensible acquires names. Our modern bureaucratic system maintains this name-giving tendency when confronted with a difficult problem. Things are better understood when they are filed.

Fixed Thought Values

In different circles of society different values are attached to thoughts. Every member of a given society unconsciously accepts this hierarchy of thinking. He shows little appreciation for the thought systems and logic of other circles. Just as the followers of Hegel detected the dialectic triangle in all' situations, so the hyper-orthodox Freudian is forever seeing the Master's patterns without looking for new ones and the Communist is eternally searching for Marxist explanations. These fixed thought values are most pointed among our common citizens. Their thinking is primarily formulated by professional interests. Butchers think in meat values, dairy-men in cheese values, psychologists in mind values, and so forth.

Private interests, especially, rule the laws of thinking. The nonsensical delusion or the illogical thought system is more often than not the justification for personal gain or material profit. "Whose bread one eats, his word one speaks" (Dutch proverb).

The delusion clearly relates to the size of the purse or the extent of political power of its propagator. As James indicated, "Truth is the cash value of ideas." (9).

The Readiness for Truth

The inner resistance to real thinking is often a violent one. Many prefer to stay in the childish dreamland of ignorance to escape the responsibility of wrong knowledge and wrong actions.

Psychotherapy has taught us how unsteady our readiness to accept truth can be. The subject defends himself continuously against painful truths. Most people have a blind spot for truths which relate to their own life and personality. This unwillingness to know disappears only after the subject is trained in self-knowledge. Such awareness causes many a painful conflict. Its avoidance, therefore, is understandable. With diabolic dialectic and ceaseless rationalizations any truth can be disguised. Only in the depth of unhappiness, in which delusion and illusion are more painful than reality, does the preparedness to accept the truth about oneself come about.

Personal relations toward truth vary. Some change their personal truths constantly. Imagination and myth are often stronger than truth. Archaic images are forever regaining possession of reality.

Knowledge—A Dangerous Game

People with too many arguments should always be approached with suspicion. Dialectic and endless reasoning are usually used as resistance against disagreeable truths. Knowledge and insight can be dangerous. The adept may be persecuted when he knows more than his teacher. In scientific circles, students who try to free themselves from scientific tradition are treated with much aggression.

Wherever doubt arises, compulsive thinking is used as a defense against hard truths. People lose themselves in the great problems of life to avoid facing problems of their own; they become pseudo-philosophers in order to escape the activities at home.

Synthetic and Analytic Thinking

There is a cry for synthetic thinking, especially among certain psychological schools. Those who did not dare to accept analysis as a therapy, used "synthesis" as a catchword. Analysis and synthesis, however, can never be separated in living thinking. Wherever psychoanalysis dissects arising thoughts, spontaneous synthesis takes place simultaneously. The surgeon dissects and analyzes living organisms, but the "vis medicatrix naturae" synthesizes and regenerates the tissues.

Whatever human beings divide, nature brings together again. Good analysis stimulates spontaneous regeneration. Life as such is always wiser than the human being who thinks about life.

Autistic Thinking

The phrase, "autistic thinking" is lifted from psychopathology (Bleuler). It was known that thinking could serve as a means of escape into fantasy, into the inner world which was neglectful of all outer contacts. Obstacles are fantasied away. Longings and strivings assume the aspect of reality. The subject no longer verifies reality; he surrenders to the dream. We speak of pathological autism where the escape into phantasy and dream life violates all contact with reality.

Autism is due to a lack of identification. Human sympathy and feeling for somebody are dependent on identification, so necessary for social relations. The autist abandons the instinctual roots of his existence, the common roots with other people.

All intellect and pure thinking tends to become cold and isolated, devoid of feelings and drives. Isolated intelligence creates hesitancy. The danger of the break-through of the isolated instinctual impulse is greater. A healthy character requires the integration of thinking and feeling.

Primitive thinking, on the other hand, although constantly directed toward the material world, is enslaved to that world. It is bent to the dictatorship of the sensual impulse; it does not think but acts in shortcuts. Autistic thinking is inwardly directed thinking, thinking which lacks the awareness of reality.

Thinking seems to move between two extremes: the archaic thinking, which is slave to the impulse of reality and autistic thinking, which is dependent only on impulses of the subject. Archaic thinking is introjective thinking, autistic thinking is projective thinking. In the latter, the outer world is burdened with the fictions of the subject. Both extremes lack the agile contact with and facing of reality.

Thinking can be overstrained. It cannot function without stimulation from the unconscious. Without relaxation and rest it breaks down. The mind wants sleep, it has to retreat from reality to dream life in order to regain new strength for confrontation on awakening.

Delusion and the Subjective Feeling of Power

Delusion gives the subject an inner certainty of omnipotence and strength. Normal thinking about reality is never as secure about itself. The rigid thought is stronger than man. The deluded man likes to suffer for his delusions. The quarrelsome, especially, never stop exciting and moving the world in the service of their overburdened feelings of justice. He who is possessed by delusion is forever running his head against a stone wall; the realities of logic and physical relations are of no consequence to him as he searches for the perpetuum mobile and the square of the circle. Scientific thought is irrelevant. The deluded goes his own way, growing within the delusion and anxious only to live for the peculiar aberration of his thoughts.

Thinking is the constantly expanding function of accounting for and being responsible for the subject in relation to the world. Where this process of growing consciousness stops, delusion begins. Every fixation in growth gives rise to abnormal phenomena in thinking. Real thinking, real adequatio cum re, requires perpetual conversion and renewal.

Delusion and the Subjective Feeling of Certainty

The more primitive man is, the younger he is, the more keenly he feels his opinions and notions. His experiences are for him of great reality value. Characteristic of growing consciousness is its grasp of the relativity of personal insight. It experiences doubt and hesitation, becomes familiar with the various phases and levels of thinking, with the eternal need for correction and evolution from old to new insight.

The delusion, however, is certain of itself. Regressive thinking knows no doubt; it does not see the conflict between its own opinions and reality since it is incapable of a critical self-corrective attitude.

The Incomprehensibility of the Delusion

Medical theories assumed that the delusion was intangible in terms of understanding and comprehension. Understanding is a subjective process and its degree is dependent on the individual student. The deeper the regression, however, the less contact and communication takes place, for Delusion speaks another language. Its archaic language is rooted in the period when no verbal communication between human beings existed, as we experience in the psychoanalysis of schizophrenics. A deluded man is essentially a lonely man.

Gaining insight into a delusion demands of the analyst the same temporary degree of regression the patient has undergone. But usually the intuitive artist alone is able to turn back that far.

SECTION NINE

Thinking—The Overstepping of Limits

In daily life, thinking moves on very different levels. Most people do not like the cataloging of reality. The road from random, disorganized thinking, to patterned thinking, to free intuitive thinking is not a simple straight line. Man must always struggle for a new world outlook. Thinking is a challenge and a daring feat. When we assay to leave traditional paths and step into the obscure, reality suddenly assumes new aspects. It is impossible to grasp these with old modes ot thinking. Gaining consciousness implies the shedding of old realities through expanding freedom and conquering new realities.

Growth from infantile to adult thinking is bound to the laws of physical power and matter which set limits on growth possibilities. To live is to create. The creative living subject develops to a thinking subject. The comprehension of the thinking subject includes some knowledge of his limitations. The psychology of thinking and deluded thinking must indicate the limitations of human thought in any given period of its evolution. It must indicate the origin and extent of these limitations and the means for surpassing and conquering them.

Living thought must always bypass these limitations.

How much truth can man bear? How much truth about himself can he bear? Does he have the courage to penetrate ever more deeply into reality? Can he free himself, if he so desires, from it?

Thinking must undergo a continuous process of renewal. Unless it does so, man remains only "wise". Being wise in the vulgar sense of the word means being prudent and neutral, means hesitation and keeping to the middle of the road. Man, however, must step beyond this.

Dimensional Thinking

Many thought images cannot penetrate the thought world of our fellow beings. As the rainworm lives in a world of rainworms, and a child in a world of children, so the man lives within his own thought world. His thought organs are attuned only to a special wave length. The thought pictures received are translated into his own language. Man cannot grasp dimensions which are not commensurate with his own mental capacity.

Primitive ideas cannot absorb more complex ones. Advanced thinking can, however, absorb less differentiated thinking. These differences in terms of thinking constitute the major source of misunderstanding. Human beings live in different thought worlds.

Those who live on a higher level detect the delusions of those on a lower one, but remain unaware of their own. Lower, less differentiated levels of thinking regard the higher ones as exaggerated nonsense and an incomprehensible "secret cult". Higher levels view the lower ones as regressions, delusions or disturbances of growth. Let us not forget, however, that every higher form of thinking, every truth, is the end process of the integration of more primitive modes of thinking and partial truths.

The world is full of misunderstood thought. Isolated thinking can refine itself and reach new truth; it can also, however, regress and deteriorate. In an isolated culture thinking ultimately regresses. (See section on collective psychosis.) Thoughts need intermarriage and opposition.

He who abandons a higher culture for an isolated lower culture also reverts to primitive archaic thinking. Many examples can be cited of natives who studied at western universities and embraced our form of thinking, but on returning to their former tribes shed their newly conquered fields of thought.

Nearly all of us are encased in our own world of thought and find it difficult to move beyond. We maintain the illusion of understanding a higher world but remain hemmed in by our traditions. However, all of a sudden we experience momentary flashes of insight and higher clarity and then the struggle for a new way of knowledge may start.

The Conceit of Thinking

People are hard to convince of the incorrectness of their thinking. The majority are fixated to their own thoughts to such a degree that they are unable to listen to those of others. They fear doubt and close their ears. They approach their ideas as doting parents approach their children. They fight for their ideas as Don Quixote did; they will follow a doctor's prescription quite passively but will deny the logic of his argument. Pedantic thinking is unable to correct itself. Its conception of state, society and leader are unassailable, inspired by the infantile assumption of the magic power of thought.

Chaotic and difficult thoughts are easily accepted if they bear a semblance of learning and sophistication. The incomprehensible has a strong magic influence. People are very receptive to quasi-profound ideas and abstruse demonstrations. They suspect the clear and simple. Some people enjoy the weekly sermon only when it is obscure and incomprehensible.

Our age is ready to embrace the highest truth with the smallest brain, unaware of the impossibility of the task. This constitutes the exalted delusion of technical man.

Over-Strained Thinking

It is dangerous to overestimate the capacity of our brain. When it attempts too much it overstrains itself. It does not dare to confess to its ignorance and limitations. The strained thinker not only claims to understand all that is illogical and inimical to his culture but out of his fear of misunderstanding begins to court and love what he cannot grasp. He identifies himself with absurdity. Many traitors and turncoats in wartime were themselves victims of this treacherous attitude of the intellect.

The incomprehensible, the chaotic and abstruse holds a strange fascination for many. Identification with powerful psychopaths and chaotic fanatics may result in a complete surrender of personal insights. The most abhorrent theories are proclaimed as understood and accepted. Vague fear, especially, causes this passive surrender. A similar process occurs in the primitive: he always attaches more importance to the obscure than to the clearly observed. Less differentiated thinking never can grasp more differentiated ideas. A broad abyss separates these worlds of thinking. In the Middle Ages the more differentiated way of thinking was called heresy and black magic and many clear thinkers finished their lives on the burning stake. Even now there exists a tremendous suspicion in the world toward clarification of ideas.

The Delusion of Justification

Such passive acceptance of ideas gives rise to the delusion of justification. "Look," one calls, "I think so objectively and righteously that I even plead against my old friends and fatherland." Cowardly opportunism is always destructive. It is the cause of much disloyalty and treason.

Everyone can prove with abundance of pseudo-arguments that the immoral is moral. This inner treason begins with the vague acceptance of the small percentage of truth which shields a big lie.

Thoughts can have a narcotic effect. They can sweeten every sorrow. There are philosophies for periods of success and periods of failure.

The liberation of one's thinking from archaic chains is a hazardous process. The path of the spirit is narrow; the fear of a vast vacuum tempts many to throw themselves into the abyss and to surrender to the dark drives of the unconscious.

A philosophical system can be justification and delusion. There is a tendency to escape into ivory tower philosophy and empty theorizing out of impotence. That is why so many philosophers in Germany became easy prey to authoritarian suggestions. Those who referred to themselves as lovers of wisdom turned easily into philosophers of the mailed fist.

The Treason of Our Thoughts

Let us go back to the treacherous delusion of justification. What is this curious need to betray the father and teacher? Is it only the mental reaching beyond the own being and the own period? Or is it always mingled with hate and resentment?

In times when our soul is empty, we sell ourselves for a couple of poor ideals and we become traitors, too. Much treason and crime arise out of shame, guilt and powerless reproach for our own inadequacy. We heap coals of fire on our own head. Out of an inner shame of ourselves and others we destroy what we love and honor.

There are other forms of disloyalty, however. Deep in our soul lives that other form of self-betrayal, the regression, the tendency to revert to more primitive opinions. Regression of thinking and advancement of thinking are both considered betrayals of the conventional systems. There is high treason and cowardly treason.

Real treason, however, can only be a self-betrayal. The problem is that of the potential traitor in all men. It is the process of justification of the fundamental dissatisfaction with oneself. People who like power politics can misuse their insight. When one's existence becomes vulnerable, one's thoughts follow suit. Thought control is the new technique of suppression of the authoritarian state.

The danger of a huge corps of civil servants is that a highly intelligent group becomes dependent on a salary. Their thinking is gullible and much too conscious of their dependence on governmental power.

The Mania for Objectivity

Thinking that is strained—and in times of chaos all thinking is—becomes receptive to relativism. Spiritual values are no longer accepted and the personality is not involved fully in evaluations. The thinkers begin to schematize. They are unaware of the tensions of life. The rigid thinker begins to hate what he does not understand. He argues more than he acts and loses himself in senseless dialectic. He betrays himself. Through talk he sets the wrong right.

Many people suffer from an objectivity disease. Objectivity assumes the proportion of a compulsion neurosis. They refuse to choose between contradictory ideas. They lack the passion for further and better thinking. Beware of those who remain objective and dispassionate. They betray the ever-developing continuity of life. This pseudo-objectivity may also be treason. Life is a constant choice between right and wrong, between going backward and going forward, between the primitive and the civilized in us. Those who insist on objectivity do not dare to chose and betray the good action that had to be chosen. In a world which suffers, to remain a spectator is a luxury and a shirking of responsibility. "Objectivity is to expose and to lose oneself." (Bolland).

The last war taught us well how many a so-called objective thinker became a collaborator of the enemy. There is a form of intellectualism which is sterile, which surrenders easily to power. Intellectualism differs from intelligent productivity. It is imitation without creation. Our world pays too much homage to such unproductive learnedness. Real intellect is a potential apart from knowledge and pedantry.

Every man, for fear of becoming a consequential thinking being, is a potential traitor. He often talks and argues for fear of expressing himself and coming into conflict with reality.

Thinking demands patience, attention and the gradual development of consciousness. The destruction of old wisdom and productivity is not always free productivity. Not every rebellion is a sacred revelation. Wisdom grows in the weak as well as in the strong, in silence as well as in conversation. But silence may be treason when there is a need for the thinker to speak.

Delusion and Resentment

The greatest disappointment in thinking may be when there is lack of energy to express itself. Ideas are too often tired. The danger then arises that the disappointment becomes dogma, that the half wisdom is seen as a final product.

The disappointed thinkers compensate for their impotence by erecting immature theories. The uncultured myth is then launched on mankind with the help of the fist, if necessary.

Much rancor and resentment motivate thinking. It constitutes a kind of mental auto-intoxication. When there is no energy for coming to terms with the world, the compulsive stream of thought is directed inward and destroys the own mind. Hate and resentment grows in the mind and directs all thinking and action.

Nietzsche in his "Genealogy der Moral" explains that this becomes the way in which the weak and the slaves obtain the means for the moral and mental oppression of others. Resentment denies all that is different. Resentment causes prejudice, persecution and revolutionary chaos. Through nihilism and stupidity it masters the thoughts and exercises thought control over others. Yet it survives with the delusion of creating a higher culture.

Resentment destroys all that is spiritual. The failures in life, those who feel ignored, revolt against the thoughts of their time and turn hate and rancor into the highest wisdom. When the fist of the enemy lay heavily on our occupied country many unsuccessful thinkers used the situation for spreading their weird opinions with the help of the guiding hand of the conqueror. There was no freedom and argument was forbidden. Idealistic catchwords disguised the thinkers' resentment. The thinker with the fist will long be remembered in the memory of occupied nations.

Pathological Delusion

In the nineteenth century there was a tendency among psychiatrists to explain pathological delusions in a mechanical way as an unclear electric current, a short-circuit of the brain, or as an intoxication of the normal stream of thoughts. Delusion and thinking, however, are integral parts of the living organism and the function of coming to terms with reality. Every thinking process is rooted in a primary vital process. Those who refer to the delusion as a partial reconstitution of disturbed thinking are correct. In every living function we find regression and progression beside each other.

The important problem in reference to delusion is why normal man is able to correct the slight delusions of everyday life while the mentally ill are unable to do so. Delusions as such are normal symptoms as long as they are subject to correction. The primary delusion among psychotics is incorrigible and the same is true of the affective delusion among depressives.

This raises difficult questions in psychopathology, namely the "why" and "how" of delusions. They may be the result of tiredness or vital debility, of intoxication, of putting out of circuit certain nervous centers and elements, of repression of drives, of general regression, of unbearable conflict, and so forth. This etiological approach, however, does not explain delusion as such.

Delusion is a disturbance in reality confrontation and in the continuous alert function of consciousness. Delusion is an isolated thought development. Delusion is an idea that is split from the continuous process of thought-integration. That is why normal contact with reality and the environment is disturbed. There is no longer any growth, reciprocity or dialectic development. There is only a convulsive congealing of archaic thought processes. Thinking means living; losing and finding oneself. The deluded is incapable of that. He regresses to archaic thinking processes, to magic, projective and autistic thinking. The deluded has given up the struggle for a *common* world picture. He is unable to participate in social thinking.

Normal thinking, too, forms illusions and delusions, but these dream pictures remain in contact with reality. The rigid delusion has lost this integrating contact.

Because the delusion is incapable of integral and agile thinking, it gives rise to a subjective feeling of certainty. The delusion is not subject to discussion. The delusion has lost the attempt at self-correction.

Being alive means maintaining contact with reality. Delusions are not alive, for they lack the vital doubt which raises life to a higher level of consciousness.

The delusion does not only originate from within ourselves but also comes as a suggestion from outside, as we will see in the chapter on mass-delusion.

Thinking Needs Harmony

When thinking becomes detached from man, when feelings no longer impregnate the thoughts, then thought processes arise which take hold of man and drag him into obscure depths. When knowledge does not go hand in hand with love it acts against man. It becomes a weapon in the service of the beloved ego and a murderer of others.

Correction is possible through conflict and crises. A slight delusion is at times necessary to arouse people out of apathy and inactivity.

Every delusion starts as a form of expansion. When the delusion becomes fixed, however, it is a pathological process.

The value of thought is dependent on the personality behind it. Propaganda of a criminal with ethical formulas is worthless. The same words can disguise different hearts. For some, they may be a delusion; for others, the expression of a harmonious, well-integrated personality. The one idea may hide the most destructive drive; another idea may be the expression of a personality who stands by his words. This is the only criteria we have for evaluating delusions.

II. MASS AND DELUSION

The Problem of the Mass

Following the first World War much interest was devoted to the problem of mass thinking and public opinion. The fighting powers had taken great pains to influence the masses and involve them in the armed struggle. Mass propaganda, press censorship and thought control became important areas of concern.

Until then, only a select group of sociologists had devoted attention to the problem of mass psychology (Le Bon, (11) Sighele). After Versailles this interest spread among literate peoples. Books on the subject began to appear. The general public had experienced the ecstasy of war and the decline of civilization and now turned to reflection. The politicos, now familiar with the notion of mass-psychology, also began to raise certain questions.

Before 1914, one could not really speak in terms of mass opinion. People remained aloof from world politics and most were taken by surprise when the war broke out. The preceding years of peace had established a deep belief in the stability and essentially peaceful nature of twentieth-century man.

By 1918, all this had changed. Simultaneously there arose an ardent idealism and belief in new world peace, and a cynical view of mankind and its problems.

The realization that people's thoughts and beliefs were significant was a sudden one after the war. The masses had fought the war and were ready to play a role in the shaping of the future. Even the dictatorships became concerned with the nature of public reaction. A respect developed for mass opinion.

Mass psychology has the potentiality for becoming a dangerous science. Like mass technology, it may be used as an instrument in the service of criminal powers. That is what happened under the Nazi regime. Nazi psychology strove for the most effective utilization of social organization in the service of evil and anti-social powers. Nevertheless, no government can function without some knowledge of mass-psychology.

The science of the masses was further enhanced by the closing of the world's frontiers. Mankind can no longer escape into uninhabited or unexplored areas. This is why the problem of mass grouping is increasingly coming to the fore.

Catchwords such as "herd-animals" and "mob rule" only serve to obscure the problem of the mass. Since the science of mass-psychology can so easily become a political weapon, it is difficult to keep it free of catchwords. For this reason we speak of a dual trend in mass-psychology: on one hand, there is a positive mass-psychology concerned with the evolution and progress of different social formations; on the other hand, there is a negative one, concerned only with the regression and corruption of the masses. (German psychological warfare was a good example of that perverted application of psychology).

The Molding of the Masses

Mass is derived from the latin word "massa", "that which can be molded and kneaded." Improved techniques of communication make the mass more subject to influences than ever before. People are in closer contact with world events. They cannot be shut out from the world of politics, when kings and presidents appeal to them over the radio.

A study of mass delusions need not necessarily concern itself with specific mass-devisions and formations. The psychologist is primarily concerned with the identificatory tendencies in every individual, that which lives as "mass" in every individual. Man, like all animals, leads a double existence. He is at once a unit, an individual and a part of the world that influences him. The world of his fellow-beings assumes a major role in his existence. There is individual closeness and collective communication. The individual grows as part of his community. The most adamant individualist cannot withdraw from collective influences. One is mass even when one is alone, through identification with different collective phenomena. One may identify with a leader or with its humblest members, with its symbols or its written rules; one always becomes a virtual part of them. One becomes part of the mass by reading a newspaper or listening to the radio, or even by preparing a speech for a meeting. Mass means a state of collective relationship and interaction.

Mass is not only a horizontal concept—a relationship with one's contemporaries—but also a vertical and historical relationship with one's ancestors and kin. We identify with parents and ancestors, with the history and tradition of our country and race.

The collectivity has tremendous convincing power. Our arguments are unconsciously fortified by joining a fictitious majority. We swear by the "communis opinio". Especially during periods of emotional stress we feel the need to be part of a majority and to lose ourselves in its anonymity. By so doing, we compensate for personal wants. "If we can't do it alone, perhaps the mass will succeed." The collectivity as such has more élan vital.

Mass Thinking

Public opinion has always been molded in the service of special aims. A lie repeated ten times becomes believable, and one repeated a hundred times exerts a hypnotic effect. All propaganda utilizes this psychological experience to imbue the masses with subjective truths or lies. Intelligent reasoning does not carry much influence with the masses. The unorganized masses think in terms of their simplest members. Organization and training gradually raise the level of isolated collectivities and formations. Mutual and collective training in thinking advance a group beyond its own limitations. A mass ideal can inspire the individual to achieve beyond his own capabilities, since the feeling of unity with others gives a sense of greater power.

Every individual is simultaneously subject to different and often opposing communal forces; the one retards; the other advances him. Although no generalization is possible, individual creativity occurs in the interrelationship with the collectivity. Man, however, is not entirely the product of the mass. He is a distinct unit, reacting in a differentiated way. Through working and thinking with other people, through a joint search for truth, genius begins to flower. This requires organization, however. Such groups, for instance, as clerical orders or study groups, have evolved the kind of social-thinking which refines and civilizes itself through patient training and cooperation. Where people work and think together, a democratic atmosphere develops which stimulates the individual, and every form of conscious organization of the mass brings about through its affective ties a gradually maturing intellectual relationship.

The mass as a crowd, as an accidental formation, however, does not undergo a similar process. The reaction of the mass depends on its organization, its formative ties and its cultural level. Where there is no seeking and thinking on a communal level and mutual relationship, thoughts regress to the stage of collective primitive thinking.

The formation of "mass man" as such results in decreased individual fear and lowering of the mental level. A mechanization of the soul takes place. All men are partly mass, that means: object of collective influences.

The mass binds individuals and equalizes them by exerting an archaic authoritarian influence on their critical faculties. When the mass becomes more self-conscious, as in a democracy, that unconscious authoritarian attitude disappears.

The uniform reactions of people toward collective symbols, similar to the common symbolism in dream life, permits us to speak of common unconscious emotional ties between the individual and the collectivity. With Jung, (10) we can speak of a collective unconscious and collective thinking. Collective thinking has unlimited memory. It is easily influenced by suggestion and lacks all critical capacity. Collective thinking wields tremendous power and influence. The unorganized masses make the same affective adjustment as natives in the jungle. Words and thoughts assume a magic significance. They become catchwords which evoke mass-feelings. They are meaningless and unverified but act as emotional signals which arouse hate and aggression.

The collectivity also has its unconscious life and dreams. Every revolution, every war evokes that collective dream. Certain collectivities forever cherish the dream of revenge or power. Alongside their conscious display of power lives their magic-mythical state. Some collectivities eternally stimulate and arouse memories of something great, of a hidden kingdom of dreams. It is curious that in the mass soul as well, there exists a polarity: the conscious wish for order and planning stands in opposition to chaotic dreams and ideals. There are people (and nations) who lose themselves in this tragic split.

As individuals we are moved at the deepest level by the élan of the collective unconscious. The mass as such does not create, but it provides vital energy for the creating individual. Man often loses value when separated from the collectivity, when he lacks what he can introject and assimilate from the group.

Mass thinking is a living reality within us. It bears more resemblance to feeling than to thinking. Real thinking, real coping with reality takes place in isolation, but the collectivity delivers the emotional energy to it.

When a native comes into contact with our civilization he learns to think in accordance with our mores. When, however, he returns to his tribe, the old collective concepts again take hold of his mind. When a German meets a German, the German myth begins to work with him; when two Dutchmen meet each other, the consciousness of their past is revived; when two boys from Arizona get together the spirit of the Western border becomes aroused.

The Craving for Catchwords

The constant repetition of an emotional symbol makes the masses ripe for government by catchword. The catchword can precipitate the discharge of a specific collective explosion.

After the Germans had conquered Europe by arms, they tried to conquer its spirit by catchwords. Their friends the traitors and turncoats knew the trick well. Whenever they had the opportunity, they coined new catchwords to obscure the old ones. They were fighting for the most beautiful ideals. Such phrases as "The New World" and "Fighting for a New Europe" were common ones. "Renewal" became a particularly dangerous catchword. Whenever the fallacious implication of a catchword was exposed, a new one was coined to justify the old ones. Aggressive catchwords enabled the masses to express and discharge their feelings of hate, and each man could project his private angers on the mass-invective.

The Equalization of the Masses

The mass leaves no room for particularity and individuality. The individual must learn to howl with the wolves. Mass thinking intimidates the individual. Only a very few are able to withdraw in critical isolation. The mass challenges this withdrawal; especially when a general feeling of fear prevails is all non-conformist thinking forbidden. The equality of mood acts as a narcotic; the individual is finally dragged away by the feelings of the mass. The catchword and the spirit is assimilated. One is forced to scold with one's fellow-members at the official scapegoats. The excited mass demands substitute objects on which it can discharge its disappointment and fury. These serve as cathartic agents.

Almost instinctually man is forced to cooperate with and yield to the mass. It becomes impossible to evade mass-thinking and mass action. The first impression will determine whether we will conform or not. The need for direct evaluation forces us to give in to conformity.

Traditional Mass-Thinking

We develop as an organic part of the collectivity. During our development a process of mental assimilation takes place in which habits

59

and traditions of our environment are unconsciously absorbed. They grow within us and we cannot rid ourselves of them. Adolescence engenders a certain intellectual opposition which evaluates old patterns of thought and action and which may even lead to non-conformism. Nevertheless, the traditional idea, intellectually and critically conquered, suddenly comes to the fore.

Man is bound to different social circles and formations. Sometimes those different influences may clash in the individual. Everyone who enters a certain group or social formation assumes, consciously or unconsciously, its rules and traditions. Against his will he assimilates the language, the gestures, the prejudices of the group. He takes over, too, the archaic forms of thinking, the superstitions, the taboos, the delusions of the group. Jung referred to these unconscious assimilations as archaic engrams and innate ideas.

Conformism and Submissiveness in the Masses

Among certain groups of animals, leadership is determined by the animal's physical prowess. The animal who, by force or accident, wins the struggle establishes its position of leadership. The champion assures not only his leading place in the group but also the submissiveness of the others.

We all submit to certain forms of supremacy and leadership. The tyrant fascinates us into obedience. Subconsciously we follow him even if our mind revolts. In every community a continual struggle for precedence takes place.

Especially when a mass is on the move, we must obey, as if in panic. Following and obeying provides a comforting satisfaction. This is particularly evident among children and soldiers.

The last decades have demonstrated how the masses, under the influence of criminal propaganda, can become criminal and primitive. Medieval witch-hunting is revived. Minorities are persecuted and slaughtered in gas-chambers. Injustice is tolerated, accepted and even justified. Mass delusion converts every member of the mass to a criminal. This form of mass-universality, as imitation of the leader, still fosters shame and guilt-feeling. It is the minor "criminal vanguard", however, which fascinates the mass and changes its moral laws. A pseudo-unity is formed through fear and fascination which must always be perpetuated with further fear and fascination.

The Paradox of Censorship on Public Opinion

When, after 1918, the science of influencing the public became more systematized, the chaotic attempts at psychological warfare during the first world war were studied. Governments established departments of press and propaganda.

Napoleon already had recognized the importance of taking such measures when he established a "Bureau de l'Opinion Publique". Following his time, the interest waned.

One of the chief problems centered about the means of methodically deepening the unconscious docility of the public and deriving the utmost profit out of this submissiveness. Propaganda and influence always carry an authoritarian connotation. Public opinion becomes a keyboard which may be played on ad libitum. The soundness of this psychological technique, however, still remains an open question. Propaganda techniques utilize sentimental methods of expression which play upon the emotional resonance of large masses. The pretense of tears makes others cry. Every psychologist, however, is aware that these expressions disguise other feelings and other intentions. The pretense of conformity is not equivalent to thinking in conformity.

The first propaganda attack leaves the public rather unsteady but continual suggestive pressure brings about certain immunizing processes. The individual is able to build up his mental defense. Gradually people retrieve their critical faculties. Popular character and previous collective training decide the sensitivity of a population to propaganda. When the propaganda has a flattering effect on the minds, when it provides justification without hurting the self-esteem of the mass, then it exerts a great influence. Propaganda for war, for instance, has to discharge the conscience of the people. Intellectual motivation in such instances is subordinate to emotional justification.

Finally, however, a general critical attitude comes to the fore. The alien propaganda, the nerve war launched by the enemy, has little effect. The suggestive armor of the enemy never reaches the people. Only under terror will it temporarily have its effect. During the first World War, Germany paid millions to purchase the pro-German opinion of the world. Public opinion, however, is much more independent of propaganda than one supposes it to be, as may be seen in political contests where a free voting public rejects candidates backed by powerful and influential forces.

Not only do controlled press and propaganda lose full contact with public opinion, but they also achieve a paradoxical result. The greater the censorship and the more suggestive the dictatorship, the more the people will seek other means of verification. The broad mass is well aware—though not always consciously—whether its information is dictated or free. Dictated illusions are often accepted because they conform to the wishes of the mass. When, however, this conformity is absent, even truth is interpreted as lie. During the last two years of the second World War, German propaganda artists had to fight constantly against the catastrophic interpretation of their "victories."

As early as 1936, unsuspected Nazis were attempting to obtain foreign uncensored newspapers. They borrowed the papers of foreign visitors, asked their opinions, listened to radio broadcasts from abroad. During the war, when the first ecstasy of European conquest came to an end, this attitude became especially pronounced. The desire to be cheated diminished in the horrible reality of bombing raids.

The danger of all propaganda is its potential power to convince all those who must deal with it daily. The propagandists themselves are most susceptible, and believe, in the end, in their own cheating. Real public opinion maintains its skepticism. In periods of censorship and dictated thought rumor and whispering campaigns flourish. People become confused by their own fearful imagination. They believe nothing and they believe all. The most improbable rumor becomes truth. All news from official sources is interpreted by means of a secret formula. During the German occupation, I assisted at several sessions in which Nazi newspapers were investigated as cryptic reports which had to be explained by special formula, giving new meaning to the words.

Man cannot accept thought control. He must express himself. He demands the right to free conversation. He is like the barber of the fairytale who was compelled to whisper his deadly secret into the ground: "King Midas has the ears of a donkey." Criticism can never be extinguished because criticism in one's own soul is not extinguishable.

Suggestive Weapons

There are, however, suggestive weapons, fascinating catchwords and penetrating formulas, which inoculate the masses so effectively that hardly anyone can escape mass-infection. Some thoughts can be hammered in with great suggestiveness. Their effects depend on the preparedness and vulnerability of the masses to mental infection. The need to yield to suggestion is all-pervasive, even in the so-called democratic countries. Democracy is easily tired and lazy and there are few who offer mental resistance. We are not trained to be individualists.

Recent historical events have taught us the results of several suggestive press campaigns. We know how radio commentators can influence the population and arouse panic. * We have experienced how lies of fictitious invasions are used to make the people ready for war. The catchword "holy hate" fascinates. The construction of an acceptable casus belli is not difficult. Even "test-rumors" are made use of to gauge the mood and reaction of a population. The dictator must forever flatter the public and test its love for him. Hitler knew how to feed the people with dream-pictures. He erected huge palaces and monuments to fascinate and flatter the masses.

Propaganda, the technical application of suggestion, contains much magic. The constant repetition of "I win" and the repeated inscription of that phrase convinces the primitive soul that victory is near. The streets and walls of occupied countries were plastered with magic posters announcing the German's final victory. The gods are induced to bring about victory by magic action. In this way, the archaic man of the glacial period conquered the bison, and twentieth century man pursues the same strategy.

Independence of Public Opinion

It is a well known rule of the science of hypnosis that suggestion can never draw more out of a man than is already in him. That is, we cannot direct the masses to war without a latent desire for war.

Experiences of the presidential elections in this country in 1936 and 1940 indicated that very suggestive anti-Roosevelt press campaigns could not sway public opinion. The same resistance to pressure operated in the 1948 election. Suggestion plus intimidation may have results. But America is still a democratic country and no large scale mental terrorism has been utilized. What superficially is referred to as public opinion is rarely anything but wishful thinking by the formulators of leading editorial policies. Even the so-called "will of the people" is little more than the successful results of propaganda techniques. Genuine public opinion is much more difficult to test. Sample polls also cannot reflect real opinion since in reality individuals may be temporarily spellbound by given influences, which are later dissipated.

Pseudo- and Real Public Opinion

There seems to be an apparent and a real public opinion. Even at election-time, when public opinion is freely expressed, real opinions

---

*Later analysis in postwar Germany indicated that not all of these influences were effective. Suggestions from the leader—even under terror—don't always sway the masses. Dictated suggestions are followed, not, however, without latent opposition and resistance.

are often disguised for security reasons or out of a herd instinct. A kind of mass-sympathy easily results in abandonment of one's own opinion. Fear devaluates self-awareness. Who has the courage to be the one-man opposition in a large meeting? Public opinion becomes little more than a dictatorial suggestion burning on every tongue if there is no chance for free expression.

May we speak of a mass or people's will? The tendency to reach a personal goal can be broken by mass influence. There is no real mass will but there exists an inhibition of the individual will by mass influence. There exists a mass-paralysis as we all experienced in the Low Countries during the first months of Nazi terror. The individual can be dragged away by the mass. But the mass can also inspire him to courageous acts far beyond his original power.

Mass-opinion polls only indicate how the individual opinions vary from day to day. The egocentricity of the public in viewing major problems is almost incredible. A wastebasket fire in the next office is more significant than an outbreak of war on another continent. When Japan invaded China in 1932 and the first rumors of an impending world catastrophe circled the globe the American press was preoccupied exclusively with the stolen Lindbergh baby. The press was unable (or unwilling) to launch a campaign for international intervention. The public did not want to see it. The same happened in 1939. It was as if the vast public tried to frustrate the impending catastrophe. In July, 1939, a British poll indicated that the public of Great Britain apparently gave little thought to war. One of its main concerns was astrology. (6).

The Formation of Public Opinion

We can look at the problem of public opinion from the point of view of the public relations expert or the politician and ask ourselves how to imbue the public with appreciation of the importance of a particular opinion or the wish for a special commercial article. Demagogic formulas and catchwords bring the masses in contact with general ideas, with special names and special attitudes. Even illogicality is a form of power. The aphorism need not be proven, provided the formula is repeated often and brilliantly enough.

Public opinion is ready to accept, first of all, all that is emotional and touching. Criticism does not come until later. First flatter the public and arouse its emotions. This was the strategy applied by Hitler (8) and Mussolini. In "Mein Kampf", Hitler speaks of the need to "imbue" the masses with fanaticism in order to gain power over them. That is, mass thought must be constantly kept in a fluid state, under emotional pressure. To lead the masses, one must provide dynamic ideals. The big danger, according to Hitler, is apathy and inertia. Frustration and fascination, glamor and success, will move the masses.

How is collective emotion formed? Psychology refers to the process of transference of feelings to the collectivity in which the individual projects his personal feelings on the collective emotion. Real opinion roots much deeper. In a community where terror and rumor reign, emotions are easily transferred. Personal criticism is non-existent. Because nothing is verifiable, affectivity increases and mass-delusions flourish.

SECTION THREE

Individual and Mass-Thinking

This essay will view mass opinion and mass thinking in another way. Here, too, we take the individual subject as the starting point. The mass-psychologist must always and everywhere deal with living people. These living men and their formations make history. It is a mistake to speak of mass-thinking. The collectivity as such does not think; only the individual thinks in mutual relationship with the influences of the collectivity. The collectivity, however, inspires comparable thoughts in different individuals and does so to a much greater extent than the individual is aware of. The idea which does not find root in the nourishing soil of the group will wilt. Individual thinking needs some social echo or it dies. A thought is as much a means of communication as the word. The need for social resonators is as great for philosophical theories as for political fantasies. Even a meeting of philosophers has the aspect of an archaic emotional mass.

The mass keeps thoughts alive and forces the individual to think in conformity. Even in isolation the individual maintains contact with the mass and keeps his thoughts within the framework of relationships with others. How I direct my thoughts, conformist or non-conformist, I am always in relation with an imaginary social formation.

A mass meeting arouses the need for conformity and conversion. The mass has a magnetic attraction for the individual. The meeting and the mass emotion evoke, even in the greatest skeptic, an archaic need for identification and conformity. Our thinking is less immune to mass-effect than we are aware of. In relation to this the following question poses itself: How are foreign opinions and ideas inoculated in the individual? How can he remain part of a collectivity and yet maintain his private opinions? How can he relate himself to other formations alien to his own thinking? How is mass delusion formed?

The Effect of Suggestion

The suggestibility of man is an inner attitude which is best understood through the study of its psychological development. An animal, though imitative, is not suggestible, because it has no consciousness of its own or of others' instincts. The animal lives in an unconscious primitive relationship between itself and the world. The process of gaining consciousness in man caused, as it were, a kind of split between the subject and the world. The developing child sees itself placed as an observing subject, an ego, confronting an outside world with which it remains in affective contact. One of these affective relationships between the subject and the world is identification, the need for unity. Primitive psychology, the primitive conception of and thinking about another is simple imitation. The Malayan call it "lattah", when as a result of fright or fear a person begins to imitate in an unconscious and unregulated way all that the other person is doing. The woman with "lattah" is completely subdued to her environment. She lives as a mechanical doll, a slave of all outer movements. We note the same process of servility in some psychotic patients.

The animistic conception of the world is full of such identifications. Inner fears and wishes are projected onto the outside world. Material objects are virtually populated with spirits and gods. The opposite process also takes place. Man identifies with the outside world in a passive way. He is immobile like the rock; active like a waterfall.

Identification and Psychological Feeling

In everyone a certain amount of this identifying attitude survives. This passive identification develops into a capacity for psychological feeling with others, for empathy, a capacity for feeling pity and compassion, sympathy and feeling of social responsibility. That is why every man remains suggestible, bound with invisible bonds to his fellow-beings. That is why he may be susceptible to feelings and thoughts from outside, contrary to all logic and reasoning. The instinct of social identification lives in all human beings, and is perhaps the beginning of charity.

Complete identification with the thinking, feeling and acting of others is a psychological process encountered everywhere. In the play of children one object serves to substitute for another, their toys replace the objects from the mature world. The hero or leader is imitated by adolescents in particular. The people of the Far East are masters of imitation and identification. A good example is that of the meditating man of Tibet who for so long identified with a Yak—a large-horned animal—that he refused to leave his house for fear of bumping his horns against the door.

We Westerners identify with the history of our country, with our civilization, with our countryside. That is why we speak of *the* German, *the* Frenchman, *the* American. The more unfamiliar a stranger is, the more closely does he become identified with the vague and generalized knowledge of his country or race.

Participating Feeling

Through identification—also called participation—the "own" personality may be completely neglected in the service of the prototype. Animals and devils, saints and heroes, can be so thoroughly identified with and imitated that even their external form may be assimilated. This is referred to as stigmatization.

Children, especially, undergo this participating thinking. They are fully possessed by the introjected personality. They are completely subdued and untouchable by criticism. All sympathy is easily converted into identification, and identification into submission and slavery. Through identification the own personality becomes eliminated.

The feeling of unity with the mass stimulates a great many people. A rhythmic march can invigorate and touch the onlooker. The feeling of participation is an overwhelming one. Identification is at work everywhere and at all times.

Not even the most critical philosopher is exempt. At the University in Leyden, a very intelligent student of my well-known teacher in philosophy (Bolland) continued the lectures of her master after the latter's death. She had not only assimilated the philosophy of her teacher, but his voice, his attitude and gestures as well.

We all undergo identification and participation, especially if we feel enthusiastic about someone or his thinking. The process of identification and participation weakens our critical attitude. That is the price we pay for living in a social community.

The Social Value of Suggestibility

This infantile suggestible attitude prevails among the mass. It is as if men withdraw their critical rational feelers. Those who aim at protecting others and becoming less vulnerable themselves by avoiding suggestibility, disregard and overlook the social value of suggestibility. The first principles of human love and charity are related to such participation. Through the process of identification and equalization the individual becomes less vulnerable. In the mass, we are dealing with people of various mental attributes. When a mass opinion, a "communis opinio" is formulated, mutual aggression is forestalled. Every individual gradually becomes part of a community and takes over its moral norms and valuations. The mass is comprised of passive onlookers who await suggestive, positive leadership to which they can conform.

Anonymity

There is danger, however, behind identification and participation. The free development of the individual may be jeopardized. Too much attachment to a collectivity inhibits personal growth. Man becomes a passive and unintelligent follower. He acquires the habit of thinking behind the pretext of anonymity. He no longer formulates individual opinions but becomes the interpreter of the thoughts of others. He is no longer responsible for his own search of truth. The collectivity has assumed that responsibility.

Mental terror of long duration ultimately reduces all people to this phase of anonymity and thought-slavery.

As mentioned above, modern techniques of communication are well able to "de-individualize" man. Modern techniques can bring about thought discipline more effectively and are also better able to control it. Man can become a thinking slave in a powerful technological organism. Technique means power and mass. Technique depersonalizes man, technique makes him anonymous. The personality always experiences resistance in the mass. Individual peculiarities are regarded with hostility.

This feeling of unison with a powerful technical will is felt by many as a liberation from individual responsibility.

Lability of Mass-Opinion

When we speak of mass, then, the mass of people with an opinion, we must have primitive and childish evaluations. We must reject all reasonable norms and think in terms of myth and suggestion, lability of opinion and primitive optimism. The mass-affect is nearly always directed against the intellectual function. The mass is suspicious of critical intelligence. It tolerates only affective relations and rejects all critical control. Even in scientific meetings, we may be subjected to the same psychological laws. The adept speaks; the audience listens in a magic spell; the fathers criticize; the critical outsider is banned.

It is impossible to generalize about mass or public opinion. Our experiences are constantly changing and constantly dependent on fear or mental terror. Every public opinion poll reveals only the cross-section of a mood or a certain mental spell.

The mass lacks all real motives or justifications. Its only value is success. It prefers to assimilate tentatively the opinion of the conqueror. The mass requires heroes and traitors for the projection of its emotions. Unconsciously, these satisfy the individual's inner desire to betray or his need for heroism.

This lability changes in character during wartime, when excesses are much more evident. Rumor and terror wield greater influence. Out of a need for self-justification the mass is very prone to follow threatening suggestions. As long as public opinion is paralyzed by fear and terror it constitutes a weak defense against terror and injustice. People are forced to sacrifice their moral norms.

A good example is the changing opinion the Germans held toward Chamberlain, England's Prime Minister before the war. Prior to the Munich betrayal of 1938, the public showed no interest in him. After Munich, he was hailed as savior of the peace; in 1939, he was regarded as a plutocratic satan. All these opinions were inoculated in the German people by the Nazi propaganda machine.

Through mechanization of the mind—a symptom of Western civilization—the mass can live a long time without any consciousness of its problems. Only crisis and suffering may arouse the minds. That is why the mass is intellectually lazy and spoiled. Patriotic ceremonials, confession, the servile press, often appease the deeper conscience and lull the people into a pseudo-peaceful sleep. After the shock of the second World War, there is more interest in general affairs. But every propaganda for noble aims has to fight against the peoples' eternal wish for sleep.

The unreal optimism of the masses during the year 1939 was indicated in a number of opinion polls. In July 1939 hardly anyone believed sincerely in war. The personal wish was the father of general insight. The bleak representations of the European press were not accepted. The German people reacted similarly. The armies, nevertheless, were gradually mobilized. Although writing about social psychological subjects, I, too, tried to negate my melancholy expectations of an impending war. I started my vacation trip in 1939 with a careless feeling of elation. Only much later I realized, through all kinds of symptomatic actions, how much I had been prepared for war and disaster.

The public and the individual as such always attempt to suppress bad experiences and melancholy expectation. During the long years of German occupation, peace festivals were repeatedly celebrated as a reaction to rumors. Even the enemy soldier was often infected with the festive spirit of peace.

In a mood of panic, especially, every suggestion is imbued with tremendous power. The wish and the fear determine all opinions. Our allies, the British, were forced to bomb our houses and towns, but the population refused to believe that its homes were smashed by British bombs. They interpreted the devastation as a cowardly revenge of the occupier.

Historical evidence of the instability of public opinion is given by the German people. Toward the end of 1932, the Nazi minority strength was waning. From March 1933 on, under the impact of Hitler's reign of terror, more than 90 per cent of the stated public opinion seemed to support Hitler.

SECTION FOUR

The Effect of Fear and Terror

The psychology of observation and the analysis of witnesses before the court teach us that in moments of emotional tension all objectivity is lost. How distorted the reports on a minor accident can be! In a fearful state every peculiar event is interpreted as an omen, and even the most common occurrences cannot be described accurately. Fear demoralizes the witnesses. They act primitively and eliminate all logic and self-criticism; they are confused and do not know how to think. They become hypersensitive to new threats of danger. If one wants to get across a particularly aggressive point of view to a country or community, it can best be done by suggesting that there is danger. The people must be frightened by rumors and threats of an enemy. Vague fear paralyzes all criticism. What the press prescribes to believe is readily accepted under the spell of fear. Suspicions toward neighboring countries increase. The vicious circle of hate, suspicion and heightened suggestibility arises.

We live in an era of suspicion. Man is weakened by fear, fright and terror. He readily accepts any catchwords and opinions which promise security. At the same time, the mass experiences a need to become familiar with fears in order to master them.

Induction Psychosis and Mental Epidemic

If the above symptoms are well understood they will be found to have a broader application than to political happenings alone. The best examples are seen in small isolated communities where a pathological fanatic, driven by exaggerated religious zeal, fascinates his fellow-citizens and makes them fearful. He injects them with his delusions, as, for instance, in the perpetration of a sanctioned religious murder. Religious murders precipitated by a collective psychosis are still not too rare. They occur in isolated villages or on small fishing boats. The threat of hell and doom by a fanatic make it difficult for an isolated community to confront reality. The collective delusion finds fertile ground for growth. The population of the ship or of the village follows the psychotic's contagious behavior, and assimilates the same delusion. Recognition of this tendency may well explain the ancient practice—in protracted periods of ill-fortune—for the group to seek out the individual possessed of the evil spirit and condemn him to death.

Mass-Delusion

When the pathological leader is removed the pathological spell seems to disappear. Every mass delusion, however intense, disappears once its cause is eliminated. As soon as an armistice is signed the former hated enemy is already seen in a more normal light. War as the deluding element is eliminated. Often the reversion takes place—all kinds of delusions of justification arise about the behavior of the criminal enemy.

Among huge masses, especially, reason can easily turn into delusion. A mass can easily become panicky and querulous. It is as if unconscious material exploded. Minor causes can ignite the intuitive flame of mass delusion through what Hitler referred to as a "fanal"—a token or signal.

Collective phenomena are less sensitive to correction than individual phenomena. Because it is widely shared by identification, collective delusion is less amendable to correction than individual self-deceit.

Contagious Mass-Delusion

Apathy, rigidity and the feeling of paralysis are likewise contagious. After natural catastrophes and war we experience collective mental paralysis. The process is the same as with primitive people who, paralyzed by hunger, become more and more passive and finally surrender completely to famine and death, even when food is not far away. They no longer make use of active defenses. Among more civilized people as well, mental epidemics are connected with exhaustion and famine. This partially accounts for the general depressive hangover in Western Europe which followed the second World War (15).

Various religious sects practice fasting and systematic bodily exhaustion to induce a state of mental sensibility and ecstasy in their followers. Ascetism furthers the formation of hallucinations; mass ascetism paves the way for mass delusion. Hungry people are dangerous. The hallucinations of one spread easily to others. The mass imagines more and more.

All these processes are dependent on cultural factors. When civilization becomes limited, tired and decadent, archaic forms of thinking revive.

Diffusion and interaction between cultures prevent mass delusion.

Short-Cuts and Mass-Delusion

In mass delusion all coming to terms with reality is lost. Argumentation is inverted because of the intellectual laziness of the masses. "Because Negroes are lynched, something must be wrong with them. Because witches are burned, their souls are sold to the devil. Because Jews are persecuted, they must be evil." Pity the wolf that has a bad smell! Very few will be willing to free him of that smell.

The study of mass mental epidemics explains the changeability of the masses. Perhaps it is more difficult to cause mass contagion among more civilized people. Yet, on a ship it is only necessary to call "shipwreck" to cause collective hallucinations of drownings and wrecks.

As with the neurotic, the collectivity, too, has its unconscious complexes which may be stimulated and brought to the fore. The mass is highly affective and is governed by rather simple feelings. Only minor justifications are necessary to evoke mass explosions and mass murder. These are brought about particularly easily when a state of fear already exists. Mass delusion provides more emotional satisfaction than logical criticism. The collective delusion is the common catchword, the token, on which all private longings and needs are projected temporarily.

The collective symbol provides everyone with the necessary satisfaction. Paradoxically, mass delusion, rather than being an impersonal phenomena, provides everyone with an opportunity to abreact his private wishes and phantasies.

Historical Delusions

Mass delusion and collective psychoses were already clearly observed by the Romans and Greeks. Think of the mystery-cults whose members assumed all kinds of ecstatic attitudes which climaxed in epileptic convulsions. Similar orgiastic dances are still found among members of certain tribes. The Greeks sometimes referred to these as contagious satyr-delusions. The possessed suddenly began a dance which culminated in an epileptic fit. One possessed dancer influenced another until the entire mass was involved in the orgiastic dance. Thus, it was believed that the satyrs in them awoke. At the end, people fell down exhausted; some even died.

Mass-Delusion and Rite

Every rite restores men to the magic realm of infancy. As soon as a club is formed, such rites are performed by its members. The cheer of a football club, the ritualistic gesture of a political group, the masonic rite—all these signify the magic longing for a dream country, for returning to a blessed state that has passed.

In the mass, where one's anonymity is preserved, unconscious drives are much more easily discharged. The cult and ceremonial are merely justification for this deeper process. Token forms of similar regressions can be observed at a masked ball, for instance, where the mask and anonymity facilitate regressive behavior.

Chorea-Major, St. Vitus Dance

The mass epidemic of dance fury during and after the first World War is still fresh in our memory. The same phenomenon could be experienced during the second World War. The dance is of tremendous importance as a simultaneously binding and freeing element for primitive mass groupings. Through dancing and orgiastic behavior the masses tried to escape their primitive fears of the gods. Plutarchus described such an epidemic among the girls of Milete. When rumors of the Black Death (plague) reached them, they burst into furious dancing, showed all kinds of ecstatic attitudes and finally committed suicide. The therapy for such behavior was curious; when these girls were threatened with being dragged naked through the streets—dead or alive—the mass-psychosis disappeared.

Toward the end of the 14th century a contagious epidemic of dance fury swept Germany and spread to all of Europe (St. Vitus Dance—Chorea Major). It followed the Black Plague. The victims of the epidemic broke into dancing and were unable to stop. Many cloisters were infected with this so-called "chorea Germanicorum". In Italy the same process was referred to as "Tarantism" and explained as the result of a toxic bite of a spider, the tarantula. The exalted dance cast a mysterious spell. The spectators were carried away by ecstasy. It was generally believed that the dance had a cathartic effect. It could heal and liberate from depressive and angry moods. Special melodies were composed to influence and soothe Tarantism. The melodies as such caused ecstasy and exercised a hypnotic effect.

History records many similar motile mass-psychoses as reactions to fear, war and persecution. In individual pathology the same form of abnormal defense reaction is known as "fear mania". Following a frightening experience the patient shows an apparently cheerful exaltation combined with hallucinations. Toward the end of the 16th century—the period of reformation and religious persecution—a similar mass reaction is reported for children. Following a dance, these children assumed the delusion that they were cats, climbed trees and began to meow. Driven by mass contagion, they identified completely with cats. The same is valid for the "werewolf" delusion, which the Nazis tried to arouse anew in their youth movement (14).

A well-known sect given to ecstatic convulsions were the so-called "Tremblers of the Avennes" in France during the 16th century. They were unmercifully persecuted. The same kind of motile fury could be observed later in all kinds of religious sects—the drum-dance of the Shamans, the sect of the Jumpers in Pennsylvania. Even now many a "pardoned sinner", when confessing in open meeting, shows symptoms of chorea and convulsions. The emotion is too great for the mass and among some the mass emotion precipitates an explosion.

Modern Chorea

Modern chorea has assumed another aspect. Fear still evokes restless movement among men. Modern man tries to escape his fears in the raving frenzy of automobiles and airplanes. Men does not dare to relax but is on a constant lookout for movement and diversion. Jazz and other rhythms lure people to archaic depths, to become part of a chaotic mass of sound and movement. Intoxication and ecstasy turn them into wild dancing children.

Wild auto races along the highways conducted by the Nazis in occupied territory were typical of such an attitude. The participants seemed like children trying to escape their guilt. One officer admitted that he performed dangerous racing feats to escape the tension of previous war-days. He was unable to remain quiet and seemed compelled to drive around. Catapulting along the road, playing with wheels and controls, imbued him with a feeling of power. The technical sorcerer is again alive within us. Aviators, too, know this intoxication. Ancient chorea has become the raving frenzy of the highways.

Mass-Ecstasy

Rhythmical sound and motion, especially, are contagious. A rhythmical call to the crowd easily foments mass ecstasy. "Duce, Duce, Duce!" The call repeats itself into the infinite and liberates the mind of all reasonable inhibitions.

In collective contagion the unconscious means of communication also play an important role. Certain emotional movements can be easily suggested to the mass. Think, for instance, of the contagious yawning, coughing and laughing in a theater.

The Suicidal Thinking of the Mass

There is something destructive, masochistic in mass thinking. The archaic instinct wins out. Action is preferred to judgment. It is not victory that is aimed for but the suppression of certain feelings. Heroism is chosen as a kind of self-punishment; the daring and the bold throw themselves into battle out of hidden feelings of guilt.

It is as if the mass simultaneously feared and loved panic and explosion. Some masses even long masochistically—though unconsciously —for slavery. Man in fear does not like freedom. The submissiveness of the masses is much greater than is usually supposed. National differences do, of course, help to determine the difference in degree of masochistic mass-feeling.

Mass-Suicide

Individual and collective suicide is frequent during periods of collective psychoses.* In Milete, as already described, suicides were committed after the convulsive ecstasy of the victims. In Russia, during the 19th century, religious sects existed with suicide as a special aim. Hidden collective fears stimulated such suicidal behavior. The suicidal epidemic is familiar as an adolescent symptom and is especially fre-

---

*See the second essay of this book.

quent in boarding schools, where it serves as an escape and revenge toward parents and teachers.

Following the invasion of Western Europe by the Germans a suicide epidemic appeared. Intellectuals and aesthetes, especially, were unable to defend themselves against the contagious delusion of world doom. When all living is dominated by fear and compulsion, then suicide may be regarded as a final expression of free will.

During the Middle Ages suicidal tendencies and preoccupations were exceedingly common. About the year 1000 the arrival of the Antichrist was expected everywhere with great fear. The entire world was infected with this magic fear, which led to all forms of self-torment, flagellantism and suicide—and simultaneous persecution of Witches and Jews.

The children's crusade in the Middle Ages offers the best example of mass delusion. This religious ideal provided the pretext and justification for mass orgiastic behavior, mass regression and aggression.

The Delusion of Metamorphosis and the Delusion of Witches

The delusion of being someone else is a curious one. It stems from the phase of mental development in which ego and world are inseparable and undifferentiated. The archaic thoughts stemming from that period are persistent and indestructible. The feeling of mystic participation reappears and man believes himself bound to other beings and metaphysical forces. The images of the group assume more reality than man's own critical confrontation of reality. This form of archaic thinking is still in evidence in our times. I am not I. My own value is of no significance. I am part of a crowd, a race, a soil, a school, a scientific clan. The label I wear is of greater importance than real value. I must have papers with rubber stamps and not a soul. And when I do not wear a special label I am found to be guilty of some unknown crime. This is what actually happens to our displaced people. This means, psychologically, that in such spheres the ego is not liberated from its family history or environment.

In a primitive way we find the metamorphic delusion in the fear of being transformed into an animal, for instance. The fear of one's own animal instinct stimulates that delusion. One does not dare to eat meat through fear of acquiring bestial qualities. The Middle Ages saw the rise of werewolf epidemics—the collective fear of being transformed into angry werewolves.

Once the werewolf delusion was fixed, all drives and instincts were permitted to come to the fore. The delusion became a justification for devilish disorderliness. Hitler tried to form such werewolf organizations to take over after his death. It is the artificial delusion which prepares for the outbreak of bestial instincts.

Among people with strong inner tensions, especially, the fear of an outbreak of their own hidden drives grows steadily. The cause of the fear is projected onto others, who are then accused of being changed, cursed and possessed by a magic spell. This gave rise—and still does—to the horrible delusion of witches. The witch is the recipient of our projections of lust and bestiality. Modern times have substituted other invectives for "witch".

Toward the end of the Middle Ages the burning-piles were lit everywhere to receive the witches expiating their devilish metamorphoses. A collective delusion of persecution reigned throughout Europe. Even the best were not exempt from the delusion. Cattle were believed to be poisoned by witches. Citizens were cursed with a spell by the followers of the devil. Children were slaughtered. The judges took part in the same delusion. Few could escape the mental mass-contagion. In Holland—thanks to the influence of the psychiatrist Joannis Wier—the last capital punishment of a witch took place in 1597—two hundred years before many other countries. Where the phenomenon of delusion becomes better known, the persecution of witches and other "possessed" victims is stemmed.

None of these delusions are too far removed in history. Until late in the 19th century the deluded man brought his human offering to the altar of his primitive gods. In 20th century Germany these delusions were again revived. The burning-piles were lit again, the gas chambers set in motion, God Moloch and other tokens of human delusion again assumed their human flesh. The Jews became the new witches.

The Delusion of the Ritual Murder

The Romans accused the Christians of drinking the blood of slaughtered children at their ritual suppers. Confessions were extorted under torture. In the Middle Ages the same ritual murder was projected onto the Jews, and in Russia the ritual murder myth persisted until the Revolution of 1917. The Chinese, too, accused Christian missionaries of fabricating magic ointments out of children's organs. Over and over again we find that unconscious primitive habits are projected onto scapegoats in various parts of the world. Projection of one's own criminality takes place everywhere, as though the accusation partly satisfied personal bloodthirsty longings. The best example of these primitive projections are found in the Nazi publication "Der

Stürmer" in which the Nazis consistently stimulated and encouraged primitive urges.

Criminal fantasy prefers to accuse other people.

Collective Conceit

Primitive mentality enhances the feeling of personal worth and conceit. Slight delusions in relation to others are very common in man; he is forever trying to shape reality in accordance with his wishes.

A higher sense of reality furthers the awareness of one's place in the universe, in the community and in the family. The primitive tendency to make oneself more important, however, is a difficult one to conquer. All primitive tribes have gods which are more powerful than neighboring gods. They consider themselves chosen and preferred by their gods, and this sweet delusion makes them love their own importance.

The collective delusion of being a chosen people is not characteristic of the Jews alone. Every people believe in their own superiority; when they are powerful they accept it as a matter of fact, and when they are weak they must needs proclaim it. Some psychologists refer to the collective delusion of superiority. It seems as if this delusion enables a collectivity to be creative and to reach a higher stage of civilization. Collective cohesion as such stimulates feelings of superiority. A feeling of inferiority makes the collective passive and defeatist. The colored races, as well, have their theories and delusions of superiority (more vital, more musical, more long-suffering). All people know this delusion of superiority. Success is suggestive. Men bow to success and make it the yardstick of their moral evaluations.

The same conceit is found among Mohammedans. The British, too, have a strong feeling of superiority—"right or wrong, my country." Patriotic attitudes concerning the American way of life also express this general feeling of superiority. Let us never forget the horrible implication of the quite naturally accepted myth of the Aryan race. Here the feeling of superiority becomes a delusion of greatness which has already precipitated collective madness.

Scientists, too, may be infected with feelings of conceit. They may not be aware that even science is weighted with affectivity and emotion. How many new discoveries are scoffed at in the beginning because they run contrary to the "official" school of thought. The relation between the will to power and science, especially, leads easily to feelings of scientific superiority. Just as in the Middle Ages, this may result in the prohibition of free research.

Take, for instance, social research, a science so near to political interests and power politics. No social scientist lacks prejudice or is free of preconceived feelings and intentions. It is easy to make social science the servant of power politics in a non-democratic state.

The Readiness for Collective Delusion

If a leader or a party tries to alleviate collective feelings of inferiority and if the leader is not a sound personality, he can graft nearly every mass delusion into the group. If one eulogizes the glory of one's own people or race, the humiliated immediately feels himself raised. The envisioned glory of the proletariat raises the poor to new action but also to new delusion.

It is significant to note that the Semitic group, with the most persistently maintained delusion of greatness, became, because of its persecution, the champion of law and justice. The weak always revolts against the strong under the banner of justice. However, the idea of justice is already a correction of the delusion of superiority (15). The passion for justice can correct the idea of superiority and teach the people more national and racial modesty.

Collective Symbols

When primitive mechanisms come into play and mass-thinking penetrates our thoughts our thinking becomes impoverished. Talk and argument are substituted for thinking. Primitive mass attitudes always have an authoritative effect. They prescribe what has to be thought, while the fear of the spiritual and soundly intelligent gradually grows.

In times of chaos and diffusion, especially, everyone hopes for the satisfaction of his own private instincts. The claims of the unconscious drives, which were previously placed under censorship, are transferred to the generally accepted symbols—the State, the Army, the Leader. These must satisfy the unconscious longings of the masses.

All are eager to accept new symbols and tokens, keys to the fulfillment of their secret wishes. A new mass delusion is born out of the meeting of unconscious wishes. Everyone projects what he personally longs for most.

The Germans were careful to formulate such symbols and phrases for the populations of the occupied countries. The word "new" was used with particular effectiveness and therefore, became immediately a suspect word. The "new epoch . . . new future . . . new blessing for mankind" were suggested as symbols of a fulfillment of hidden childish expectations.

Propaganda for the "new" does little beyond offering old wine in new barrels. Real new thoughts do not announce themselves as such; new ideas first grow in hiding. They reach the light through the warmth of our burning need for truth and insight. New thoughts and new feelings cannot be imposed.

The Power of the Masses

In the midst of all kinds of fearful, magic imaginations the masses long for greatness, for symbolic fathers, capable of furnishing security. The masses demand powerful fetishes and powerful kings. They want to be subjects of a powerful state, which can praise and punish, hate and revenge.

The lust for power is always a primitive fear symbol. It is the fear of another's greatness. It reflects the primitive alertness of the herd. Thinking man learns to understand that life as such can be powerful—even more powerful than death. He does not long for external power but for the essentials of life. He has learned to relinquish power in exchange for civilization. Modern want for power and might is still a regressive symptom of a fearful mass, frightened by the economic struggle and by insecurity.

The Urge for Equality in the Mass

The mass demands equality of feeling in its members. Those who deviate are not accepted. Chauvinism rejects the antichauvinists, and a collective evaluation of beliefs is sought. Symbols, too, express this collectivity of feeling. The symbol works as a deceiving sedative which affects even the outsider. Everyone learns to run with the pack. The collective cry awakens something in men, of which they were hitherto unaware.

It is not the idea, the original thought which affect the mass, but the catchword, the token, the symbol. The idea is converted into a catchword and mass delusion through constant repetition. The catchword becomes a psychological weapon of power, as many general elections have shown us.

Word-Sensuality

The word has taken possession of the mass. It has converted the amorphous mass into a fixed formation. Not the idea, not reality, but the formalized word, the phrase, reigns supreme. The word "fascist", for instance, does not suggest a human being. For one man, it is a label for an ideal for which he must die or murder; for the other man, the quintessence of all that is detested. The word serves to hide personalities and theories behind indices and empty names. The words are treated as objects rather than experiences. I am often asked for my political label or my scientific beliefs. What and who I am does not matter. People want to know the school I attended; the books I quoted or the way I voted, never what I really think.

When the word is expressed energetically, its power is enhanced. Quantity overwhelms quality. The word becomes loaded but loses meaning. We all make use of loaded words, of "blab" words, with such broad meaning that they no longer convey anything. It is one of the diseases of intellectuals that they are more concerned with words than with real concepts.

When the word loses in real content it gains in magic and acquires the mysterious ambivalence of primitive words. Like the words in primitive languages, catchwords connote either confirmation or denial. Ministries of propaganda—factories of opinions—are masters in the fabrication of sweet justifying words. They can create—as Goebbels did —beautiful phrases for the most horrible crimes. If the mass is ready to accept these, it becomes invincible and impervious to moral opposition.

Mass-affect is often proof of a deep valuation. In mass-affect the ego and its environment are not separated. One scolds the plutocrat because secretly one longs to imitate him. Respect and jealously are discharged in a new catchword. In every word lives such an ambivalent root. Every conscious expression of a word has unconsciously an opposite meaning. In this precipitation of opposite unconscious motivations lies the deceiving power of the catchword.

This is particularly true of generalizations. Words such as "freedom" and "justice" seduce us to a pseudo-exactitude, while unconsciously we have completely different associations. The emotional significance in the background is often more influential than the real significance of the word. After the rape of the Low Lands the Nazis overwhelmed us with the word "justice"; we became sick of it.

Twenty years ago, the word "socialist" was a nickname, while today it is the catchword for an ideal world order. "Communist and anarchist" still are, for a great many, derogatory symbols; for others, symbols of liberty. No one is concerned with the political and economic theory behind the word.

A good catchword can explain all that is inexplicable. Recently, the phrase "historical task and duty" has served as justification for all manner of immoral deeds. The suggestion of historical root finds unlimited approval, especially with the non-historically minded—and that is the vast majority.

The Dictatorship of the Printed Word

As young children, we are already overwhelmed by the printed word. We learn to believe unconditionally what is printed in books. The critical attitude is developed gradually, but the first infantile impression persists. The delusion of the printed word takes possession of us. During the occupation, the enemy flooded the occupied nations with an avalanche of printed matter. He sought to drown the evidence of his injustice in ink.

The word wields unlimited influence in the community. Preachers, lawyers, teachers and politicians thrive on the word. To oppose an opinion or fight an idea one constructs a critical phrase, a slogan, or a scapegoat word designed to reach and stir the mass. During election time in particular, one makes acquaintance with the suggestive power of empty words. The mass demands more than reality; it clamors for the emotionality of the word and the feelings that it stimulates. Politicians make use of political fetishism. Recall, for instance, all the touching catchwords and slogans of past wars. What remains of them? —"Mare nostrum", "War of revenge", "War to end Wars", "Atlantic Charter", "Asiatic Monroe-Doctrine", "The Four Freedoms", "Holy historical rights", "The Allied Nations", "the New Europe", etc., etc.

Mass-Hypnosis

The masses are rather easy to hypnotize because of the action of suggestive words, the cooperation of common unconscious longings and the increased suggestibility of a group. If the leader is a good hypnotist he can play with the masses. There is in the group an increased tendency to identify with the leader which makes it even easier for him to hold people in his grip. His word is our word, his "yes" is our "yes". That is why there is also an increased tendency to follow uncritically. The leader can count on increasing submissiveness of the masses, as Hitler mentions in his book ("Eine Erhohung der Hingabebereitschaft der Masse"). Because the mass is receptible to hypnotic influence it tolerates all kinds of excesses by the hypnotist. The easiest technique is to work with special suggestive words, repeating them monotonously and boringly. From time to time one has to add a few jokes. People want to laugh. The macabre, especially, attracts the masses. Tell them horrors and let them gather together in sensational tension.

When the hypnotic effect weakens, the mass can easily act against the leader. However, we must be aware of the fact that we cannot stimulate in the masses what was not latent within them.

It is difficult to immunize people against mass-seduction; they sleep too much even when they pretend to be awake. They are not clearly conscious but think circularly, jumping from one opinion to the other. This is why it is so much easier to hypnotize them than to give them a critical approach. Repeat again and again your simple motto and the many half-sleeping beings follow you passively.

Especially in times of crisis or approaching war every conversation is a repetition of a previous one. Inspired by fear and rumor, the same theme is repeated with many variations. People make themselves more and more suggestible and finally surrender to the feared idea.

They all act like sleepwalkers. I would like to make critical searchers out of them, people who are awake, but they prefer sleeping, the pure vegetative life of the embryonic mind. The Nazi conqueror wanted to inoculate us with a new philosophy, with a new conception of the world. He knew that for all these mental sleepers he offered a better sedative, which would make them even better followers. In Germany, only a small minority resisted. They recaptured their own mind after a long period of hesitation and after defeat of their fatherland.

Mass hypnosis lulls people into a deeper mental sleep than ever before. Mass hypnosis can convert the civilized being into a criminal sleepwalker.

There is no intrinsic difference between individual- and mass-hypnosis. The more the individual feels himself part of the mass, the more easily can he be hypnotized by individual treatment. Primitive people and primitive communities are particularly sensitive to hypnosis. Everyone knows how select individuals—sorcerers and magicians—wield a hypnotic influence on the entire community. A parallel situation prevails in religious sects where the leader can arouse at will a state of mass-ecstasy in his followers.

Hypnosis as such is comparable with cataleptic trance in the individual, the archaic form of paralysis, in which the individual builds powerful defenses against fear and other external influences. This defense reaction—occurring outside consciousness—is a general biological defense comparable with camouflage reactions in animals. The more primitive the organism is the more easily the state of catalepsy is brought about. Hypnosis makes the individual more archaic in his reactions and more sensitive to influences from without. Among Malayan people we have shown some excesses of this fear reaction known as Lattah. The frightened person is compelled to imitate all that other people are doing.

Suggestive Association

Mass hypnosis tries to penetrate the minds through the association of pleasant feelings with simple slogans. This is the secret of all propaganda. A war picture displays flowers on rifles. A cigarette brand is put across with pictures of attractive girls smoking and smiling. The enemy is labeled with dishonorable adjectives.

The masses are caught in fixed suggestive associations. The acceptance of one such suggestive association leads to another. Every struggle against delusion must first be directed against authoritarian suggestions, against propaganda, against the fear of criticism.

The Spread of Hypnotism

The success of hypnosis among highly developed people is due to the imperfect separation of ego and environment. No matter how high the civilization and individualization, the ego and the non-ego are never completely differentiated. Only in our clearest moments of consciousness do ego and reality stand in opposition to each other. Partial identification is forever taking place.

In everyday life all kinds of human qualities are unconsciously influenced by animate and inanimate objects. Our minds are full of songs and melodies, of movie stars and sport heroes. Suggestive epidemics are constantly exercising an influence. The critical ego doesn't find its place anymore. When the mechanism of identification is functioning effectively, man surrenders more and more to all kinds of collective ecstasies and their seductive influences. The good hypnotist, therefore, must himself have some archaic capacities which he transfers to whomever he wishes to lead.

Most people are easily seduced by welcome suggestions. In states of collective fear they search for the most acceptable suggestion.

In addition to those who are so sensitive to outside suggestion there are active individuals who are only sensitive to suggestion from within. We can differentiate between allo-suggestive and auto-suggestive people. Yet the latter group aims to transfer its thoughts onto others. The auto-suggestive individual first searches for a seductive dogma, an acceptable philosophical conception of the world, before accepting other influences. The allo-suggestive individual does not need to undergo the same initial process of justification.

Hypnotizing Noises

One can learn the technique of mass hypnosis through the study of individual hypnosis. Sudden fright, fear and terror was the old hypnotic method utilized by dictators. The fearful fixation on a symbol, the flag, the mass regulations, places the mass under the spell. Certain archaic noises fascinate men and keep them enthralled—the tom-tom, jazz rhythms, the military march, the intonation of a celebrated orator, the national anthem. These are seductive and fascinating and deeply moving. There exist revolutionary and erotizing sounds, captivating the audience in their spell. Rhythm has always exercised a seductive influence on the mass. It stimulates and unites, and transfers all kinds of mass-emotions.

Sound and word are good vehicles for transference. The word, especially, can make a mass-man out of us. The radio has enhanced the power of the word. Even when I am alone with my talking radio I am united with the huge mass of other listeners. Modern mind—its unconscious portion in particular—is molded by radio and advertising, by the slogans which are constantly reiterated.

Hypnophilia

Mass meetings exercise a magic influence. Music, noises, applause, speeches—all these cast a spell over the mass.

Most people are hypnophiles, anxious to daydream and sleep through their lives. That is why they easily fall prey to mass hypnosis. Archaic longings are aroused in them. The lengthy oration or the boring sermon weakens the listener and makes him ripe for mass hypnosis.

The same effect is brought about through monotony—the monotony of marching and singing. Hypnophilia arises in all those who are subject to drilling and training "en masse". We find it among soldiers, students, officers, and religious dogmatists. Even the fine arts are usually enlisted in the propaganda machine.

The mental terror and hypnosis caused by fear is tremendous. A terrorizing minority is able to keep the mass caught in suggestions which cannot withstand scientific criticism. Argumentation, nevertheless, does not help. Delusion is an archaic, malignant growth, which continues to flourish despite operations. It has its own destructive power.

Wartime teaches us the paralyzing effect of fear on human opinion. Soldiers living in constant expectancy and fear are easily infected with delusion and hallucination. We have many examples of fire panics, in which an imagined attack touched off a real counter-attack against the black empty space.

All of Europe was in a similar state of panic throughout the duration of the war. The fearful masses were ready to accept any and all suggestions. A state of uncritical vulnerability to delusion and rumor existed. The mass has still failed to recover from this inner confusion to formulate its own opinions. (15).

The War of Nerves

Wars of nerves or mental wars serve to weaken mass opinion through fear and fright. First the enemy is brought into a state of latent panic. One's own country is, meanwhile, injected with suspicion toward the enemy. As a result, the war itself is experienced by the population as something tangible, a delivery from fear and delusion. Fearful expectation is felt as more frightful than the horrible reality itself. The war of nerves paralyzes the mass. This is why the mass tolerates so many evils in the world. This paralysis of the people occurred following the German invasion. After a period of three months, however, resistance began to materialize. Inner defenses began to function again. The underground and the resistance movement sprang into motion.

The war of nerves exploits the fact that man is the animal who can suffer most, who can tolerate most, with death as the only limit.

Collective Paralysis

Collective paralysis in reaction to fright and terror warrants further analysis. The pathology of war offers the best examples. Front-line fighting penetrates the mind very deeply. No soldier can escape it. We speak of shell-shock, anxiety neuroses or combat-fatigue in the extreme cases. In reality, however, all who have experienced the horror of war are changed by it. In one way or another, everyone builds a defense against the frightening experiences. (16).

Fear and terror, before penetrating deeply into the mind, require an incubation phase before they cause inner explosion and neurotic reactions. People are at first rather passive in battle. They can fight like automatons before the inner rebellion begins. At that moment the shock reaction comes suddenly to the fore. The incubation period may last from months to years. The fear penetrates even while defenses are built. Years after the war, the battle neurosis may come to the fore.

We all know the rather emotional silence of the veteran who is reluctant to divulge his battle experiences. In the field of literature it was only after 1927 that authors began to write about their real war experiences as a last liberation from the horrors. Years after the armistice, extensive war writing made its appearance.

Restitution of Free Opinion

Fear, fright and intimidation may pass through a long incubation period and have extensive after-effects on human thinking. The human brain is heavily burdened, and much time elapses before the personality again finds itself.

As members of the mass, people initially accept the maddest conceptions. Unless they do so they feel themselves banished, isolated, shut out from the love and praise of their companions. If the terror is great enough, many a technical philosopher will hasten to conform to mass-thinking. The mass does not tolerate outsiders who confront it with a mirror of primitive pictures. The voice of freedom has to be strong in order to start again free independent thinking. In wartime, the Allied radio propaganda took very good care of that.

SECTION SIX

The Sense of Mass-Delusion

Throughout history we have experienced waves of mass delusion which threatened more mature forms of mental life. It would be incorrect to interpret these delusions as solely "pathological". Even disease as such has sense. Disease furthers new defenses and may cause a complete change in the physical and mental structure. That is why the physician uses artificial disease to overcome the fixed defenses in chronic diseases, to renew the resistance of the organism.

Much mass delusion is caused by the mental convulsions of the community. It is as if the culture has to pass through a delusional stage in order to reach new possibilities and to shed old fixed forms. Civilization can be destroyed by delusion, but it may also renew itself through it. That is the revolutionary implication of all that is pathological.

In the true sense of the word there exists no isolated individual thinking. The individual himself is mortal, but throughout his life he is the recipient of immortality in the form of cultural concepts. Man lives in and through culture; he is both a historical and an immediate being. He gathers his knowledge from the past and adds to it. Through the mental relationship and communication with his fellowbeings he becomes part of a growing culture. Mass-thinking, then, is the passing on of civilization to the individual and his simultaneous contribution to it.

A strange nostalgia and unchecked archaic drives continue to live deeply imbedded in everyone. The man of the twentieth century worships the rough beast in himself. He values power more than culture. The mass-man of Germany declared: "I draw my gun when I hear the word 'culture'." At times, civilization bows to brute force.

Years later, free opinions wins out over the terrorizing opinion. No matter how complete the terror, the paralysis is eventually broken. How quickly this is accomplished depends on the particular character of the people. Submissiveness is more characteristic of one than of another culture complex. Mass suggestion deals with people of completely different character structures. One is more susceptible to hypnosis than another.

The Stability of the Mass

Alongside the labile thoughts, there exists a stable opinion, a special pattern of living which is rooted in unconscious drives. The pseudopublic opinion becomes superimposed on the real one. Rebellious and revolutionary ideas are the pendular movements of a stable mass.

Through intensive contact, as happens, for instance, in psychoanalysis, one learns how differentiated the thinking of common man is. There are many common patterns, taken over from the environment, but there are many original ideas as well. The individual leans to differentiate between suggested and real insight, between advertised and self-conquered opinion.

The opinion of the common man is unanimously directed against terror and dictatorship but also against the political anarchy that rules the world. Nearly everyone recognizes that human reason and experience will have to build the new foundations of the world. Peace talks are preferred to wordless war and battle. War, however, also brings doubts of logic and law and justice. Very quickly, however, many reassume their old beliefs. During fright and terror the group with deeply-rooted religious dogmas thinks more stably, as we experienced during the period of occupation. Although the dogma defends against lesions from without, danger and confusion from within are still possible. Such was the experience with puritanical religious groups. The fight for freedom in the underground aroused dogmatic doubts and initiated new inner struggles.

The forced influence on public opinion, the mass propaganda, advertising, the attacks with terror and delusion, appear to be paradoxical weapons. Short-lived, straw-fire enthusiasm is easy to arouse. Public opinion, however, is a weak and unstable possession. Those who are swept away by delusion can turn very quickly against the hypnotizer. Only those who are converted in a deeper sense go through the fire of their own free will.

People can be temporarily educated to an apparent mass opinion. Such education will only be effective until the rebellion against the oppression of free thought has concretized. Thinking and stable thought patterns which are conquered after long struggle become immune to suggestive and aggressive propaganda. However, the individual must be repeatedly mobilized and immunized against his suggestive lability and weakness, in order to counteract receptivity to delusion and mass-delusion. This we may call the quintessence of democratic action. The wisest government is one which defends man and the collective against its own stupidities and mistakes. A free man builds barriers against his mistakes. His ideal is self-control.

To free oneself from delusion means self-knowledge, knowledge not only of one's active deeds but also of one's hidden motives.

Every man is mass. Delusion and archaic thinking can therefore take possession of his mind. Human thinking is never completed. It must always reformulate its conception of reality; it must always expand. Man must grow together with changing reality. In this evolutionary process, he must offer resistance to the archaic remnants in his soul. He must become aware of the creative unconscious forces which form his thought patterns.

Objectivity toward the world can only come about through a certain degree of inward objectivity. Man is the mediator between two spheres—between the objective world and the subjective inner experiences.

When any one of these spheres acquires too firm a hold over his mind, man becomes prey to error and delusion. He is no longer himself and his hands act apart from his real individual being.

Mass-Suicide and Atomic Fear

PART TWO

MASS-SUICIDE AND ATOMIC FEAR

Is there any imminent danger of mankind exterminating itself? Is there such a thing as a hidden desire for the doom of the world?

Among ants, in the insect world, mass reactions of this type do exist. When they are forced by great danger, ants surrender to their fate. The same insect reaction may occur among human beings. If this burden of fear becomes too great, man passively gives himself up to the danger feared. In war and famine, this form of apathy and mass-paralysis is very well known. We have all heard about such fatalistic and suicidal reactions, occurring in the more emotional mass-panics. Examples were reported from the front in Flanders in 1917, from Caporetto in 1918, when huge armies in chaotic panic surrendered themselves to fear and death. And from the battlefields of World War II come numerous examples of mass-suicide. For example, a report on the taking of Saipan* describes a Japanese officer cutting off the heads of his kneeling men with his Samurai sword; crowds of soldiers and civilians jumping off the cliffs or wading into the ocean. Others were said to have blown themselves up with grenades after first playing ring games with them. "Three women sat on the rocks leisurely and deliberately combing their long, black hair. Finally they joined hands and walked slowly into the sea." A hundred sailors on the rocks at Marpi Point bowed to the Marines from the cliff-tops, spread a large Japanese flag on the rocks, then pulled the pins from the grenades that the leader handed out.

We have a tendency to dismiss this "mass hara kiri" with the explanation that it belongs especially to Japanese rites. Yet the same tendencies—although they are more concealed—do exist wherever there are masses of people.

Latent Suicidal Thoughts of the Masses

In all unorganized mass-action and mass-thinking, there is something destructive, something masochistic—a hidden drive towards defeat and doom. In general, in every sudden mass action, primitive instincts begin to dominate; primitive aggression and destruction are preferred

---

*Reported by Lindsay in *Tribune*, London, August 1944.

over civilized judgment. The individual within the mass at war wants not only victory; he also wants to suppress certain disagreeable feelings which his burden of civilization has created in him. He chooses heroism and aggression not because he is aware of the higher cultural aims he must defend, but because he wants to escape the dissatisfaction of a civilization which frustrates him. That is why becoming a warrior holds such appeal.

It is as if the masses love and fear war at the same time. They like panic and explosion, because these explosions fortify certain heroic and ecstatic herd-feelings which people still possess.

Man in fear does not like freedom. In men and among masses of people there exists a submissiveness which reaches much deeper than is generally supposed. Great national differences, of course, do exist; but the basic tendency to yield is universal in our culture. We have seen many examples recently of how submissive and cowardly masses of people may become in different dictatorial countries. There was nearly no rebellion in Germany against Hitler's criminal tyranny.

The Children's Crusades afford the best example of mass-delusion and mass-possession. During the Crusades, when the knights of Christendom flocked to Palestine to save the Holy Land from the infidels, there was also a curious parallel phenomenon. Bands of ragged youngsters marched through town after town declaring that they too were on their way to the Holy Wars. And wherever they appeared, children, infused with their hysteria and ecstasy, ran to join them. The story goes that they accumulated an army in this strange manner, boarded a ship—and were never heard of again.

Here the religious ideal was mostly a pretense and a justification for mass-orgiastic behavior, for mass-regression, and for releasing urges towards aggression and destruction. Behind all this lay the tremendous urge for self-destruction, which arose out of unrecognized feelings of guilt. The religious ecstasy was discharged in chaos and self-destruction.

In nineteenth century Russia there were several peculiar sects, e.g. the Skopts, whose special aim was suicide. All forms of rebellious ideas and hidden religious fears stimulated this suicidal behavior.

Suicide is known, too, as a symptom of puberty. Epidemics of suicide have been reported, for example, in boarding schools as a means of escape or revenge towards parents or teachers. This theme has been dealt with in fiction. In *Hatter's Castle* the little girl hangs herself to avoid confronting her father with what she considers her own failure.

After the Germans invaded Western Europe in 1940, something like an epidemic of suicide took place. Particularly hyper-intellectual types (not only the threatened Jews) were unable to defend themselves against the contagious delusion of the world's doom. When all of living is possibly only on the basis of fear and compulsion—thus they thought—suicide is our last freedom.

In cultures known to history, these suicidal epidemics crop up from time to time as abnormal expressions. But among many primitive peoples suicide is a normal expression of an accepted cultural pattern. In certain Polynesian groups, a standard method of punishing a person who has wronged one, is to destroy oneself. In other societies, suicide is so common a behavior that a tribal member who breaks a taboo may not even have to kill himself. He merely goes off by himself and dies, as if automatically. In such cultures the suicidal tendency becomes strong when the failure of aggression and attack fortifies feelings of guilt. Primitives believe that their failure is caused by a magic punishing power. Fear of the unknown and mysterious punisher forces a passive surrender to the mighty, a surrender to death.

These same feelings of guilt exist in our own society, especially during and after a war. One who feels his own responsibility for the evil in himself, and for all the evil in the world, feels essentially guilty. This intense feeling of guilt may explain the many unexpected cases of suicide that were observed among Nazi soldiers after the occupation of innocent, peaceful countries. I lived that time in occupied Holland and could describe such reactions in my war report. (16). Among his democratic enemies, many a soldier suddenly became aware of his guilt.

Mass-suicide, however, is more than a passive surrender to fate because of a guilt reaction; it is also a primitive, mystical means of escaping into the comfort of death, in order to find a new and better life. To accept death destroys the evil and vindicates the righteous. A nation full of guilt feelings, full of unsolved aggression, escapes collapse only by exploding into war. . . . "But if the war fails to keep up its furious pace and thus provide this outlet, the citizens are left with an insoluble problem. They are in the same position as the neurotic whose personality is split beyond the hope of effective action, actions related to the realities of his environment. They are totally unstable, and they are lost in the primitive confusion in which, at the ultimate point of pressure and degeneration, life and death become one. In neurotic exaltation the sufferer dies to escape death."*

The same neurotic trends and patterns exist to some degree in all

---

*Lindsay, *loc. cit.*

men: projection of fear, introjection of guilt, and ensuing self-punishment. And war activates these hidden primitive patterns which every man possesses. The same suicidal tendencies develop even further in the post-war world: neurosis, suicide, alcoholism, morphinism, the craving for a new war—in short, the post-war hangover.

The resulting guilt-feelings are tremendous. One explosion of the atom bomb killed one hundred thousand people. There is an aftermath of this explosion. Even though people may not realize it, hidden guilt feelings about mass killing on this scale are intense. For here our conscious imagination stops. One hundred people burned in a hotel fire shocks us; but one hundred thousand is beyond our imagination.

The paradoxical reaction to these guilt-feelings may be suicidal surrender to a new war, to death. These mental reactions are fortified by the world in which we live—a world full of unknown future dangers. "Does the potential enemy have atom bombs?" we ask ourselves. "Can their rockets reach us? Are they preparing for war?"

Dangerous mass-infection of these hidden emotions is spreading. All such questions and rumors keep our attitudes on a primitive level. Hitler's War of Nerves brought about the same reaction. It is the unknown danger which is weakening us—and that is why we prefer the known danger, a new war. We cannot escape the vicious circle. "Two fighting armies form one suicidal mass." (Barbusse)

Atomic Fear

The mysterious secret of atomic power excites archaic feelings among men. Are people aware how deep the thought of a future atomic war has penetrated their dreams and nightmares? Are they also aware what paradoxical action may be the result of such an uncomprehended fear?

During the hectic days when the Germans were successfully executing their "war of nerves" I held a post with an Allied Psychological Warfare group. In those days we mapped our strategy to combat those attacks against the public nerve centers as carefully as our generals mapped their battles with planes and guns. I thought then that I had seen some pretty capable psychological attacks on the public, but none, I now feel, could outdo the postwar "atomic war of nerves" to which we are being continuously subjected.

A picture of New York shattered by an atomic bomb, a city of toppled skyscrapers and mass death, is one of the examples, sketched some time ago by Major-General Leslie N. Groves, who headed the Army's Manhattan district atomic project.

Such dire forecasts are so commonplace that they no longer make the front pages of the newspapers. Day by day our minds are unwillingly paralyzed as the thought of an atomic war and catastrophe in the near future become more familiar to us.

The general idea in the "atomic war of nerves" appears to be that fear of another war and fear of the bomb's tremendous destruction will force mankind nearer to a productive plan for peace. Daily, therefore, we are served tasty morsels on the bomb's technical and political implications—and the results if international control does "not only effectively outlaw the use of atomic bombs, but . . . prevents any other nation from getting along the road to manufacture of the bomb." And if not? Then we have the unfailing picture of man cringing under the falling Empire State Building, dying with the comforting thought that none of his family or friends can escape, either.

And so we find ourselves traveling along the perilous path of peace, led by mysterious fear on the one hand, and speculation about the unknown on the other—two notoriously bad leaders of mankind. For fear paralyzes men, and when men are afraid they hope that the thing threatening will happen to liberate them from their tension. Sooner or later, like the criminal who gives himself up, rather than bear the tension of fearful expectations, we will be inspired by fear and speculation not to walk peacefully, but to cast the first bomb at those whom we fear.

I want to represent to you the example of a suicidal reaction under influence of fear. Man surrenders to fate when he has lost all self-confidence.

> A soldier under treatment for an anxiety neurosis after an awful battle experience, is in a nursing home which is hit by the blast of a flying bomb. It may be that he suffered a slight cerebral concussion, but after a few days he feels well again. There are repeated alerts for new flying bombs but he no longer goes to the shelter as military rules prescribe. He says he feels too paralyzed, he just wishes to die, he does not have the power any more to escape from death. "Why should we try to escape in this doomed world?"

Jittery citizens often write "Letters to the Editors" in various newspaper columns, insisting that we drop a few atomic bombs on the heads of some of our dangerous former allies, and, only recently, prominent public leaders suggested that we take care of the veto right problem in similar manner.

However, these suggestions not only occur to our citizens because of fear, but also because there still exists, under the shining armor of our souls, the archaic, primitive desire for war—and for destruction as well. Men say (and believe) that the idea of atomic destruction repels them, but inwardly they enjoy the thought of the bomb's tremendous power. We repeatedly find this idea in dreams, especially in dreams of patients suffering from anxiety. Didn't our reporters express their regret that the results of the atomic experiments on Bikini were not more tremendous and sensational?

Yes, mankind, exquisitely dressed up in his civilized clothes, hides deep in his somewhat disillusioned soul the primitive dream-wish of greatness, a dream-wish that would enable him to destroy all the world with one almighty gesture, like the magicians in the fairy tales, or, translated into modern comic strip terms, like Buck Rogers who launches an electronic war with one push of a button.

Although mankind consciously denies this eternal human dream-wish for tremendous magic power, every psychologist knows how deeply ingrained that wish remains. I remember well a soldier patient of mine who had announced himself a conscientious objector, yet he was inwardly fighting with such horrifying dreams of this nature that he found himself a monster. His objections to fighting were an attempt to escape his own destructive wishes. His neurosis was caused by a continual horror of himself.

So the "atomic war of nerves," which calls on fear and speculation to make us peaceful, in reality stimulates our aggressive tendencies. And, in addition, this "war" combines with our post-war fears produce a confused combination of emotions which, having no direction or guidance, can easily accumulate until they may be discharged in renewed aggression:

First, picking our way along the prickly path of peace, we carry with us a vague but nonetheless heavy burden of guilt for all the killing on the battlefield, the killing in which we partook either directly as soldiers or indirectly as civilians. As we try to secure a foothold along that path, our minds—also those of the civilians—are still slightly fogged with battle neurosis. We remember how, as warriors, we were compelled to loosen our moral bonds on the battlefield and travel the earth hating, revenging and slaughtering. The defeated enemy paid a severe price for his foolhardiness—but we conquerors came home to celebrate. This hidden guilt reaction to war was found as a fixed pattern in the culture of primitive tribes. The homecoming warrior cleansed himself from his guilt as a killer by performing certain cathartic rites. In our modern society we don't have such a ceremonial, we are less certain of our feelings of guilt, although we find these feelings buried in the war neurosis of veterans and civilians, in the guilt feelings that are converted into glorifying speeches and war memorials, and in that particular neurotic behavior in the post-war period, that cannot stop its aggressiveness. With this form of neurosis new aims of aggression are constantly sought to get even with the old guilt, derived from the old aggression. The peace is celebrated while unconsciously a new war is prepared.

Second, we are slightly blinded on our path by a strange, eerie light that has continued to burn ever since it was first set off by the blast from our atomic bomb, when, in Hiroshima alone, one hundred thousand persons died. That light constantly reminds us that we, ourselves, unleashed for the first time the tremendous destructive power of the atomic bomb—not the vicious Huns, nor the tricky Japs, but Americans did it. We feel that it was beyond the pale of the laws of war, even though we want to believe, as former Secretary of War Henry L. Stimson (18) pointed out in his article, "The Decision to Use the Atomic Bomb", that "This deliberate premeditated destruction was our least abhorrent choice." This hidden guilt feeling is probably the reason for the tremendous interest in John Hersey's account on Hiroshima.

An example of this fear I found in the following dream image:

> A member of a bomber crew in World War II repeatedly has the same dream. He dreamt he was flying on a mission during which he must throw atomic bombs on his own home town because the enemy had secured himself in the huge skyscrapers.
>
> He saw himself flying; the sun was going down; he reached his target, dropped the bomb and started his return trip. But on the way back there was turmoil. He saw suddenly a huge mountain rising in front of him. Instead of trying to get away from it, he directed his bomber toward the black mass. A crash followed and then he awoke . . . knowing that in his dream he had attempted to commit suicide and that he had wanted to escape from this foolish and guilty world.

Third, we are looking fearfully into the mysterious shadows that beset our path, shadows of that Great Unknown—the destructive possibilities of a future atomic war. Playing with these shadows are our vague fears of our own bestial and destructive tendencies. We are confused and befuddled when we acknowledge these aggressive and destructive tendencies, for we like to consider ourselves peaceful, noble and constructive human beings. These are the nightmares we not only find in neurotics but in nearly everybody who tries to become aware of the tendencies of his own epoch. I am sure that many diplomats and representatives are teased by the same nightmares.

Fourth, we are hearing in our ears the distant rumble of war drums as the fear grows that the United Nations will fail to prevent a new war. And should war come, there is the disturbing thought that future enemies will avenge themselves on us by dropping atomic bombs on our own shores.

The confused state of mind, resulting from this combination of our post-war fears and the "atomic war of nerves," resembles that of the already mentioned ancient, just-as-paralyzing period, when people waited for the world's doom because of an undefined magic spell and mysterious fear based on some general anxiety with which the world of those days was infected.

So strong is the suicidal tendency in us that we can easily turn our technological tools and toys against ourselves. The atomic bomb means either a world government, or world suicide. Another global war with atomic missiles—and our over-technical world will be doomed!

We must realize the great danger which lies in this world-wide vague fear. For this fear will operate among us just as the strange fear of magic operates in primitive societies. Unrecognized and uncomprehended fear paralyzes the human mind, hypnotizes it, makes it passive. In this paralyzed stupor man conjures up the evil he fears; it leads him to surrender passively to fate. Inwardly he is already prepared to accept death and destruction.

The great danger for the future lies in the fact that our burden of guilt and fear may undermine our mature thinking. It is this hidden fear which motivates the newspapers to publish daily articles on the coming catastrophe; and, in fearing, they unconsciously accept the destruction of the future.

Let us be realistic! There is no adequate defense against the atom bomb. It creates limitless destruction in the target area. The only counter-action is to use the same weapon; and that means mutual suicide. One bomb only, properly placed—as in Hiroshima—is all that is required to paralyze an entire metropolis. Only a relatively small amount of material and equipment, smuggled somewhere into an enemy country, is needed to assemble such a bomb. And the next atomic war will last until the last man awaits death from exposure to the deadly X-rays.

Atomic warfare is not a war of useful strategy. The greatest and the least developed country are equally vulnerable. Technologically advanced countries are even more vulnerable. But already the weapon is capitalizing upon the ignorance and the fear of the masses.

There is another side to this problem: the infectious example of Germany's self-destruction. For what one fights against infects one's own soul. Even after this war we are still not rid of Nazi attitudes. Under the ascetic megalomaniac, Shicklgruber, Germany committed suicide in an orgy of brutality and criminal ecstasy. More than nine million civilians were cold-bloodedly killed in concentration camps and behind the fronts. Too many victims were sacrificed on the altar of madness. Not only the guilt feelings of the Germans, but the guilt feelings of the whole world were aroused by these tremendous mass murders. And it is this widespread feeling of guilt that arouses the hidden wish for self-destruction. The idea of death fascinated the Germans. The stimulation of their instinctual and animal-drives prepared them to accept their own death. Their pessimistic fatalism asked for a final upheaval before the "Goetterdaemmerung." Nordic mythology is deeply imbued with the idea of pessimistic surrender to fate, and this laid a fertile groundwork among the Germans for the tendency to suicide which spread so easily among them. They were inwardly prepared; if they failed in life, the solution lay in death. Here was more fatalism than heroism, more passivity than activity. Even though defeat be inevitable, they must die for Germany. "Und Deutschland soll leben, wenn wir auch sterben werden!" (Germany will live, though we have to die!)

The suicidal tendencies of former enemies still endanger the world. In their graves they exercise a more fatal fascination than when they were actually attacking us.

Are we to accept the challenge of technology and fight to the last being on earth? Forel wrote of the ants: "If the two adversaries are approximately equal in strength, they exterminate each other without any definite result."* Are we, like the insects, bound to our mechanical instincts?

Self-destruction

We have spoken of the masses passively surrendering to their fate, of their hidden urge for destruction. What are the manifold psychological equivalents of this death-instinct?

Self-destruction is the final expression of power. It is the last way of maintaining a feeling of being valuable and potent. Think in this connection of all the ways in which spontaneity is blocked in this world, of how growth and expression are hindered; think of all the threatening and bullying and bossing, the innumerable ways in which people

---

*Julian Huxley, New York Times Magazine, February 10, 1946.

exploit each other and push each other around. Think of all the suicides as reactions to an unfavorable environment, of all the prejudices, of interracial aggressions, of lynchings. Think of all the aggressive and destructive reformisms, the riots, the street fights, the high rate of criminality, people's wildness, their eagerness to dominate. And remember the value we place upon satirical humor; how familiar we are with fatalistic ways of thinking. All these are other manifestations —psychological equivalents—of the aggressive and destructive instinct, the death-instinct. The more life's vital impulses are thwarted, the more are self-destructive tendencies uncovered.

In the war which has just been finished, unconscious tendencies to death were repeatedly revealed. In the face of the imminent threat of death, the victims passively waited for the great destruction, as though hypnotized by their fate. Many underground and resistance workers in Nazi-occupied countries clearly surrendered to death, as it were. They became reckless in spite of all warnings. To them the enemy had become an ambivalent father figure, and for waging war against him they had to be destroyed by his hands. Even more incredible was the passivity of those who had to escape because they knew that death was near. It was as if terror and death held an attraction for them.

The Urge for Catastrophe

Man in our modern world is suffering from deep shock. He is constantly on the alert, continually waiting for an approaching catastrophe; he even wishes the catastrophe would come so that his fearful expectations might be ended. His existence is shattered—and philosophers may write philosophies on "existence" as justification for their fatalism.

Again, in the Middle Ages, this kind of mood spread along with the pandemics of the epoch (the Black Death, Plague, etc.). Fear and speculation about the unknown have *always* had a stirring influence on the human mind, making people suspicious, anxious and willing to surrender to the danger they fear. Men in general prefer the actual dangers of war to the nervous tensions of an uncertain peace which looks like a verbose diplomatic war. In psychology we call it passive surrender to the thing feared: in practice we saw that people enjoyed the big show at Bikini, in spite of its threat for the future. Many people have surrendered to their nightmares and are prepared for the new explosion because they feel too weak for a constructive solution.

The urge for catastrophe does not have to take the form of longing for a fatal shock; it may be in the form of a deep craving for a momentous change in one's life, a desire to be transported to a higher and better existence. Every personal experience of death may be the door to a revival—a catharsis and a purification. This is what happens in shock therapy—the patient is permitted partially to die and to revive again. And this is effective with many mental patients.

However—and this is the imminent danger—behind most expectations of catastrophe lurks the primitive thought that the end of the world is approaching, that the world is doomed and the apocalypse is on the way.

And man, caught by this dangerous delusion, leans passively and unwittingly towards downfall and destruction.

Once before, around the year 1000, the masses awaited the great doom, and then mystical ecstasy and aggressive chaos reigned in Europe. Today we are at the same point. The notion of catastrophe leads men to self-destruction and delusion. The suicidal urge has mankind in its grip. Even the mind is participating in killing and destruction when it condones a sneering and cynical attitude. People are unable to behave because they sincerely admire and venerate something; they kill their emotions and worship mechanical idols.

It is for these reasons that so great a danger lies in the fear that is connected with the current "atomic war of nerves"; for it may work as primitive fear did in the ancient world—preparing new explosions of aggression. Too great a fear can end in suicidal reactions in a world carried away by the sweep of its dark emotions. Of course then we would cheer about the new fight: "We are liberating the world . . ." we would say again, while, in reality, we would only be liberating ourselves from the nerve-racking tensions of peace.

Such is the paradoxical result of fear: it never defends the human being against the feared event.

* * *

However, our intelligence is still able to build a positive world, not against an atomic war and future electronic enemies, but for peace, which is always a complicated but positive construction of the mind. Destruction is not the only thing which moves and attracts human beings: we are still able to use our common sense to conquer fear.

The future danger lies, not so much in the atom bomb and the mysterious potentiality of a future enemy, as in the fact that our burden of guilt and fear and nightmares may undermine our mature thinking. It is especially this fear within us that votes for more and better armaments, that pleads for more and better bombs until the explosion comes. One of the most destructive ideas in the world today is the repeated suggestion that the coming catastrophe is inevitable. This is a negative suggestion arousing and reinforcing a primitive and magic fear, which only prepares new forms of aggression.

The world needs positive, constructive suggestions: We have to agitate not against the use of useful atomic power, but against the "atomic war of nerves", against the suggested nightmares and rumors that have, to some extent, made us blind and paralyzed mature thinking. Freedom from Fear was one of the Four Freedoms. Freedom from primitive and atomic Fear needs to become one of our principal aims for the mental structure of the future.

During the war years the best science of the age was utilized in combating the German "war of nerves". Surely, now that peace is with us, we have to use our knowledge to prevent fear and destructive speculation about the unknown future. For undermining our reason and frightening our souls leads us into another war.

This is the need of our times: we have to die and to be revived again. We have gone through death, for the recent war was a tremendous dying.

Mankind's urge for catastrophe and the suicidal tendencies of the masses, are the great hindrances to a revival. Statesmen and psychologists must acknowledge these drives in the character of all people and direct their attention to combating them. Otherwise the world will continue to wait with resignation and acquiescence for what it fears and abhors but wishes at the same time.

PART THREE

Some Mental Aspects of the Human Animal

(Remaining Young, Walking Erect and Playing Continually)

SOME MENTAL ASPECTS OF THE
HUMAN ANIMAL

A Picture of the Human Animal

Only the human animal wants to draw a picture of himself and to abide by his own reflection. No animal ever described or painted himself. Why do we want to look so much at ourself and to take distance from our own problems? The second world war has just finished, people walk about with long faces talking about the atomic era and the possibility of a future world war. Melancholy philosophers speak of the end of the world and we all feel a bit perplexed by the mechanical monstrosities which ended World War II. What will our portrait be in a couple of years?

Are we capable of imagining ourselves beyond this present mood? We must get to know the strange human animal, and perhaps if we know him well we will lose our pessimistic views fabricated by physicists and moralists full of guilt feelings. In this essay we will try to look at the human being in a certain exhilarated state, for only in a phase of ecstasy can we get an essential picture of man and his future. We will use as a basis some of the biological qualities of man: his long period of youth, his special art of walking upright through the world and the implications of his continual play.

If we wish to look at the human being in the midst of his fellow-animals, we must go back to prehistoric times. From an animal he gradually becomes a primitive man with simple tools. Later on he lives in a more complicated society and very slowly evolves from a primitive into a more or less self-aware modern being. But even as an uncivilized animal, man was already different from all other animals. What are the essentials of these differences?

We can answer immediately: His intelligence and his peculiar mental structure. You may even prefer to speak of his highly developed consciousness or, like theologians, of his undefinable soul, received from higher spheres. However, I am not a philosopher; I prefer to see man as a being still belonging to the large kingdom of animals, one of the peculiar mammalia. This accepted, we ask ourselves how he became such a special kind of animal being, capable of perpetuating human civilization further and further through history.

Man Walks Erect

If we examine man's material form we see many of the same anatomical features as in his fellow-mammalia, but we observe that he walks, strangely enough, on his hind legs. Man walks erect; he differs from all other animals in the fact that he uses only two of his legs. There is a short, four-footed, baby period when his balance is unstable, as in monkeys, but after which he becomes the upright walking king of the animals.

What does such a simple change in posture imply? What does the change from a four-footed animal into a two-legged human being mean to us? The mechanical result is that the tactical mobility and manoeuverability of the body increases. Man is the only mammal able to look all around without the need of turning and shifting his position; this is why he is able to escape rapidly in any direction. His anatomy allows him to be constantly on the alert. In archaic times this tremendous mobility and alert adjustment was of great help to him in his struggle with other animals. He had acquired a more agile strategy. In those days, man had only very primitive weapons. Especially in his struggle against the big and clumsy four-footed creatures he was the stronger because of his alertness. But his respect for the faster reactions of lions and tigers has continued up to the present. We find this respect in all kinds of tales and myths.

Man Is An Escapist

Some psychologists oddly assume that his two legs and man's ability to turn about instantly created human escapism and cowardice and the tendency to evade difficulties. Human power lies in fleeing quickly from danger. Archaic man was constantly on the alert and remnants of his archaic fear still live in us. How paradoxical it sounds . . . that man can escape (e. g., his instincts) is typical of man. A man can be a prime ascetic; an animal, never.

Man Has Instruments

A more important result of his use of only two legs is the liberation of the forelegs from the function of locomotion. In his free hands, man obtained two very convenient biological instruments. Hands and fingers are the pliable tools whose adjustability has never been duplicated by mechanical devices. Through the ingenuity of the human hand technical tools were created as extensions of arm and hand. Opposite himself man places tools and machines, he builds new images. With his hands free for gesturing, man becomes a creative animal.

However, it is not only the instrumental function of the hands that became so important. Beside the eyes, the hand became the human being's most important organ of sense. The liberation of the hands gave man two hypersensitive antennae which no other vertebrate possesses. With his hands he is able to investigate the world. This world which up to now *forced* on him pure visual images in a rather passive way, can from now on be brought *actively* inside his own mind. Hence his world grows bigger and richer, and a new universe of emotions enters his consciousness. Most of the other animals are adapted to their world rather passively, though a certain form of adjustment and modification is possible. But only the human being verifies his world and adjusts himself actively. With touching hand he begins to conquer his world; his hand verifies the visual impressions. Only the touching hand may replace the eye of the blind. Seeing far into the world is touching virtually with the muscles of the eye; eye and hand are two senses predestined to cooperate in building the proper human image of reality. As a scientific formulation expresses it, "no observation and no perception can be registered in the brain without motor verification", with the result that in play and handicraft man enriches his brain still more with a continually growing field of perception.

The world in which an animal lives has a close relation to his specific biological organization. There is a continuous and mutual relationship between the design of the animal and his environment. Every being lives in a very special world, corresponding directly to his form and function. We see this best in the insect world, where the insect is limited by his innate capacities and possibilities. Depending on his momentary function, he lives in different, unrelated worlds. A hungry insect lives only in a world of prey. The rutting animal lives only in a mating world. It is like the story of the three dimensional cube in a two dimensional flat world. At the moment of intensified functioning no world outside that particular function exist. The earthworm lives in an earthworm world, without sun and stars; the mosquito lives in a mosquito world. In one there are only earthworm things; in the other, only mosquito things. In the same way, the human being lives in a human world with human things. But unlike the animal, man can vary and change his world thanks to his hands and instruments. Man does not only live *in* his world, but he confronts the world at the same time; he takes opposition. Man makes *his* own world.

Man Lives Opposite Things

Because of man's erect attitude, he not only lives with things, but he also lives opposite them. Only man is observer of his own life. Only man has a notion of his own body separate from the world. With his hands and eyes and controlling mind he *confronts* reality. That is why he is able to deny his biological habits; his own body becomes an instrument whose drives he may accept or reject. The scientist says that his biological reflexes change into psychological conditions. Only man may see his own drives and instincts as danger. Man not only knows an externally-imposed fear, but he knows an inner fear; his own impulses may become an estranged world with which he has to cope. With arms and hands he reaches out not only toward an outside world in order to conquer this piece of reality with his magic gestures (as babies do), but he also reaches out toward an inside world; he tries to change his inner longings and satisfactions. Man lives between an inner and outer world.

Every living relationship consists of a center—the being himself in a certain function or action—and his environment. There exists a dual relationship. The center *receives* stimuli from the environment and *reacts* on the environment in order to change it. For the central being there is a "perceived world" and a "manipulated" or "cultivated world" which together form "his" world.

These two worlds are not always one and the same. An ichneumon fly, by some stimuli of her senses, pierces through a layer of wood into the larva of a wasp she has never seen before. Another wasp pierces with deadly certainty into the neuroganglia of a spider although she was never taught about the anatomy of spiders. The manipulated world changes for the animal when his biological aim changes. During copulation, his reflex behavior differs completely from his conduct during the oral incorporation of food. As the biologist expresses it: "His functions develop in different fields of action." The actions of different animals, however, become more nearly the same the closer they approach their real biological aim. The last movements during copulation, or during the incorporation of food, or during the defense against enemies, take place by innate reflexes without variety, just as we saw in the ichneumons. Such innate instincts direct most of the actions and behavior of the lower animals. However, we find the same monoform pattern of actions in the primitive reactions of men.

The Tyranny of Instincts

A nice example of instinctual fatality is seen in the behavior of procession-caterpillars. They move through the woods in long lines, the forepart of one instinctually attracted by the tail of another—hence the name, procession-caterpillar. If the first one is moved so that it touches the tail of the last one, and a circle of caterpillars is formed, they are then doomed to walk in the circle. Their instinct forces them to do so until they are liberated from this spell of reflexes. Such may be the mechanical dictatorship of innate reflexes, of innate patterns. The insect-world has nearly no variable adjustment. Man has the most varied forms of adjustment. He is the animal who can suffer and tolerate more than any other animal.

We must now consider how the human world is a function of the special human organization of innate habits and reflexes. This is an important question, especially in pathology. We can, for instance, easily conclude that only in human beings do "perceived" and "culti-vated" worlds meet. Man has notion of only one universal world. How-ever, we experience repeatedly the fact that in some forms of neuroses and mental diseases those worlds again diverge. In schizophrenia, for example, the virtual motile world of ideas no longer corresponds to the world of sensory impressions. It is as if man regressed to the old insectual split world. We cannot speak then of a perceived reality, but of a world of delusions and hallucinations. In man may appear a tragic split in different worlds—tragic because the old archaic longing, a tremendous longing for biological unity, remains.

To return to the point, we can split the perceived world of man into a far away *visible* world and a much nearer *touchable* world. We find the same division in animals, too; but in human beings we see that these worlds overlap each other almost entirely. The visual images have to correspond to motoric verifications. It seems, however, that we can-not entirely comprehend our special world through our senses of touch and our motoric verification; only when it is combined with the touch-ing antennae of the eye does our world achieve the connotation of unity.

There is a difference between our visible and our touched world. The visible world is a far bigger and wider world. However, without the control of the touching hand and the virtual movements of looking around, it tends to be too fantastic. What one cannot touch and verify remains a little uncertain. The sun and moon and stars, the clouds and rainbow and the distant mountains become gods or the homes of gods. Until technique becomes the lengthening piece in our touching hand and we can grasp more and more our universe.

The same rule applies to pathological cases; the vision that escapes the virtual motor control, the memory of the senses that cannot be verified (for example, as a result of intoxication) becomes a hallucina-tion, an impression cut off from reality.

Far more magic and free of reality is the world of that other human sensory organ: the world of things heard. Here we know no direct cooperation with other senses, unless we interpret in this way the co-operation between sound and muscles, as we detect it in word and rhythm and dance. By means of sound and word, a metaphysical world enters our ears. As soon as the separate worlds of the individuals try to communicate, word and speech are born in order to bridge the abyss between the human beings. Sounds, music and speech help to build a higher united world, the specific spiritual world of the human being. The sounds move along a completely different dimension, not in space, but along the line of time. Rhythm and music give man notion of time and eternity. Only man can *look* experimentally into the future; an animal never does.

Man Grasps the Opportunity For Speech

But also, the development of sounds and speech and words has to do with our walking erect and the liberation of our forepaws. The breathing animal is able to transform the expirational air into miraculous symbols. He transmits his sound through the air to other people. That is the beginning of animal communication. But only in human beings do the larynx and pharynx transform the air in such manifold ways. That is because the human larynx is situated differently from that of other mammalia; it stands perpendicular on the base of the skull and is farther away from it. This is a necessary condition for speech, for the varied sounds and the consonants are formed by the now bigger mouth and its motile walls. Man's first language is a gestural language of the eyes and cheeks. The larynx serves as an initial source of sound under the constantly changing musical qualities that assume such manifold forms and, as an end-result, produce the rich modulation of speech.

Speech and language come to us through the ear. The old belief: "The spirit enters the human being through the ear," seems to be quite true. Without our ears we are spiritually isolated. A blind man would be isolated from the world if he did not have a sense of touch instead. Also, it is much more difficult to find a substitute for the sense of hearing. Hence, the deaf are much more isolated from society. There is even danger that his perceived world (from earlier days) will get beyond control; the deaf man hallucinates sooner. In the blind we never find any lack of reality confrontation.

For the touching hand, the "perceived" world and the "cultivated" world merge in a three-dimensional world. Sense and instrument are united. That is one of the reasons for the reality of the touched world, and is also why a man can look outside and inside. Only man has introspection; the notion of a perceived world and a world of inner drives.

With the touching, transforming, separating and assembling hands, under supervision of the eye, man builds in space *his* world of things. This was made possible for him by his erect posture.

An Eager Learning Animal

Let us accept that walking upright is one of the fundamental functions of the human being. This two-legged animal, who has become more intensely acquainted with the world and with reality than any of his fellow animals, must, however, be able to make use of this opportunity. Certain conditions must be fulfilled before man can *learn* about that world of real things. What we call learning is the building of one's "Own world" as a result of verified experiences and innate habits. The human being is well developed in verifying his experiences. Without doubt he is the most studious animal and the most eager to learn, always busy regulating and coordinating things into his own world. This manner of conquering objects virtually and bringing them within his own horizon is one of the first cultural deeds of man. Later, this becomes his scientific method of research into reality. The human being is eager to learn, eager to grasp things into his own world, eager to annex reality. Man becomes the librarian of reality.

According to John Locke the human intellect is an empty vessel which has to be filled with experiences. It is only a potential power; nothing is acquired by the intellect, which is not gained by experience. Man, as an intellectual being, has no innate ideas and almost no innate patterns of action. His world is an experienced world.

One of the best examples of this is language and human communication. The organs of speech are ready when the child is born; the possibilities are there. Nevertheless it speaks only the native language. If one had taken the child somewhere else, it would have spoken another language and conquered another spiritual world. Perhaps this all sounds too simple, but we have to realize that man is the bearer of the civilization into which he is born. There is no heredity of culture, no innate knowledge of morals and habits. There is only a greater or lesser innate power or potentiality to grasp these things. The culture and civilization passed from one generation to another have to be learned. This is especially what Locke, who had no notion of an archaic insectual pattern of reactions behind the civilized ones, meant.

The newborn human being is without civilization but he has various means of grasping the culture of his time. We must realize that man is animal and human at the same time. As an animal he is born with

innate reflexes, with innate instincts, patterns and biological tendencies. These biological patterns of behavior can introduce many disturbances in his civilized life. When he is not satisfied sexually or
when he is starved, he does not continue to act as a civilized being; his
inborn biological patterns win over all his learned habits. Freud taught
us how the innate instinctual pattern is the deep-rooted basis of human
action and that the civilized patterns are the instincts changed as the
result of education and experience. Jung adds a more mystical explanation. He sees man as still rooted in a collective unconscious, as
part of an archaic instinctual collective being. The pattern of action
which man has learned is only the upper layer; beneath this reigns a
prelogical instinctual form of thought, feeling and action, just as they
reign in the world of insects.

Innate patterns of action are multifarious in the world of animals.
What would we think of a child being born a completely equipped
toreador, acquainted with all the qualities of the bull and the art of
plunging his sword with unfailing certainty into the right spot? This
is the norm for every digger wasp. It knows how to paralyze its victims
by one sting in the head ganglia, so that they do not die and will remain
fresh for future use as supper. Nobody taught them to build their
complicated breeding places. Their mother died long before they saw
the light of day; their father was a brainless insect used by their mother
only for copulation. They had no school, only a breeding hole with
the paralyzed spiders as food supply where their mother's eggs had
been laid. Beyond this the mother wasp has no further interest in her
descendants.

Birds are also equipped with many "innate ideas". All varieties of
birds know how to build their nests without architectural education.
Every bird seems to be born equipped with a map. When birds of pas-
sage begin to migrate, the youngsters often form the outposts and
advance guard, so that they cannot have learned the path of flight
from their parents.

Man has almost none of this innate knowledge which he likes to
call "instinct". Even in the satisfaction of his most archaic instincts
only the final reflexes are innate. He has to learn how to ingest his
food, and only swallowing is an inborn reflex. During copulation, only
the last motor act of orgasm is reflexive; only then is he pure action
and reflex, feeling the ecstasy of an innate action. But even this ecstatic
instinctual act is lost in many impotent neurotics.

How can we explain the transition from a reflexive animal to the
hesitating and delaying "learning" human being? This new cultural

process begins at that point in biological evolution when the senses cease to serve only as receivers of stimuli, which they turn into active automatic reflexes. When for the first time the stimulus results in the formation of a new adjustment, of a new pattern of action, something new develops in the organism. We call these newly-formed patterns conditioned reflexes (Pavlov). They open the way for new associations and new chains of reflexes in the animal brain, enabling it to learn. The new reflexes form new nervous impulses along new tracts in the brain and in the end those new associations form a more differentiated human brain (Neurobiotactic theory of Arriens Kappers). This experienced nervous apparatus is well formed only when the eye, hand and ear are used conjointly to build an experience, when together they form a fresh image of reality which in turn changes the form and action of the nervous apparatus.

Only Man Is Surprised

There is a moment during man's evolution when a new excited astonishment appears, a feeling of surprise at all those things which until now were accepted as normal without any reflection. This new astonished approach to reality begins to control and to verify all the materials of experience. This surprise spreads continually and the human being enjoys his expanding universe more and more. All that stimulates the senses is looked at as new and as more beautiful! The astonished caveman drew a design of a mammouth on a rock, and "caught" him with his magic creation. Out of fear and astonishment, man begins to create his own world outside the control of his senses. The child begins already to project his vague impressions (hallucinations) on the world. Hallucination and reality cover each other gradually.

Man tries to catch the world. Out of his new experiences he builds his own world. The human being is beginning to learn and to create!

Man has to learn about his own life; an animal never can. Man, because he opposes the world, has to create his own spiritual world.

Man's learning is a learning of mankind! Through learning man acquires a social heritage, a knowledge and science he transmits to the next generation. A man has culture and history. He can not only learn from his experiences—as animals can—but he can learn from history, from the experiences of early ancestors. He even learns from the animals, but animals do not learn much from him.

It must be said that insects also pass on certain social patterns to the next generation but only through a biological and genetic evolution.

Their learning process is stereotyped and is limited to the individual and to the given situation. Its learning dies with it. Man, alas, tends to fall back into those stereotyped actions.

Through collective learning, man grows dependent on his fellow beings; he only is a psycho-social being. The individual does not die; his notions and knowledge add experiences to the group. Man not only has a biological heredity, but he also has a *cultural heredity*.

Prejudice—The Enemy of Learning

The greatest enemy of learning in man, is the conviction of knowing already. There is no greater hindrance to teaching someone than his conceit about knowing already and the delusion that he is already able to do all the things he wants to do. Prejudice is the enemy of adequate ideas, and those acquired in early youth from environment and tradition are so dangerous because of their tenacity and overvaluation. We may compare them to the innate reflexes and ideas of insects. The historical pattern of action and the inborn knowledge which resides in a group or in masses form such a tenacious prejudice. They keep the spontaneity of life bound and hinder new forms of creation. The human being as a member of the masses is in such a way bound to his fellow beings. Mankind is one huge plant with many roots, many sections and many joints. No social action is possible without many members having a share in it. In the individual, awareness that a man is a joint in such a superhuman "mass-being", is often expressed in illogical racial feelings, which from time to time supplant his rational thinking. When he has to explain these archaic feelings, he appeals to a biological matrix to which he and his kind belong. Such rudiments of collective archaic feeling still exist in every human being and are kept alive by traditionalism. They are always ready to vibrate when certain political sounds come through the air. When these obscure ideas move the human being they destroy all logic, and the archaic insectual animal is reborn. The psychologist speaks soberly of regressions and the revival of archaic thinking; seductive politicians speak of blood and soil and rate and our infallible way of life.

Under the impact of such suggestions man may throw overboard all he has learned; he reverts to the innate world of ideas of the insect in him. The human insects may govern the world.

Man, The Eternal Baby

We are now acquainted with a few of the biological conditions of becoming a man. To fulfill these conditions, however, the human being needs still another present from nature. The impressiveness of his modifiable brain, the use of hand, eye and tongue would all be useless if he did not have *time* enough to build his world out of his experiences and verifications. Human life seems short, but the fact that more than a quarter of its duration belongs to youth and that his youth, strictly speaking, never disappears, gives the human being the opportunity to learn and to experience all kinds of things. Among animals, man has the longest youth.

The Dutch anatomist Bolk (5) proved in his theory of human fetalization that the typical peculiarities of human biological organization was its fetal aspect. This he formulated in what sounds like a paradox: Man is an unripened and retarded monkey-fetus. As we shall see it is as compensation for this biological fetal and helpless status, that man acquires the ability to develop his mental capacities. Human fetus and monkey fetus are born the same, but while the monkey fetus (and monkey baby) develop and differentiate rapidly into a mature animal, man remains a suckling with too large a head. Comparing the biological development of man with that of monkeys, we see that human growth is much more retarded. Man remains in an anatomical phase which the monkey soon outgrows. This is called by Bolk the fetalization of form. Several hormonal glands—all under apparent control of the pituitary gland—cause this retardation of anatomical differentiation. The juvenile form of many human organs verifies Bolk's theory of fetalization—the shape of the jaw, the fetal eyebrows, the local growth of hair, the hairless body, the shedding of the first teeth. This retarded development leads to a lengthening of the period before adolescence. It is well known that in this early period the basis is laid for the later world of ideas, images and attitudes. The experiences of childhood are necessary for the development of adult mental life and it is extraordinarily difficult to fix anything into the human brain of which the primary forms are not present in early childhood and prepuberty. The great wealth of the outside world comes to us between our first and fourteenth years, when we are most open to impressions. These years compensate us for our lack of innate ideas. The impressions of that age still have the power of innate ideas. They sometimes have the same mechanical effect as the training and drilling of animals. In many lives this unconscious drilling recurs unexpectedly just as innate ideas do in animals. A peculiar urge to repeat the early infantile patterns develop in man. In the last decades we experienced full well what governmental drilling of the mind is able to do. Thought control returns mankind to the mechanical patterns of insectual life.

We are now touching on a very curious chapter in psychology, the formation of ideas during infancy, school-age and the period of emotional latency. All that is established in the infantile brain grows in this period deep into the fundamentals of future patterns of behavior. Group behavior especially is conditioned through this process. In the post-war period we still have an opportunity to study the causes of psychopathic behavior as a result of demoralization, fear, tension, and paradoxical education through war habits.

Man walks erect, he is born naked and he is a fetus. He exposes all his organs, unprotected by fur or other armament. He is very conscious of his lack of defense and his nakedness. Man is the only animal with clothes, with shame and with the exhibitionist urge. Man became especially vulnerable in his sex organs; the opportunity of hurting them is greater than in other animals while his impulse to sex life is much more frequent and random. In no other animal do we experience this frequency of sexual activity—one of the reasons, perhaps, why so many myths have arisen dealing with man's sexual life. Greater vulnerability and greater capacity always lead to greater tension. Greater tension must lead to greater social suppression. The continual limitation of his increased sexual urge must have transformed all kinds of aggressive fantasies into action. Because of man's early and unquenchable sexual urges, because of his continual longing for unity, he undergoes a continual inhibition from outside. This may stimulate the most beautiful creative fantasies but it may arouse the most cruel destructive wishes towards the frustrating forces. Man is a homo eroticus. Erotic defense and exposure alternate. His earliest aggressive fantasies are related to the loving action or rejection by the parents. Many later forms of aggression and cruelty depend on those early imaginations. Frustrated sex and too much exposed sex—both breed aggression.

The Dreamer-Fighter

Man is not a real fighter. He is a dreamer-fighter without the biological tools. However, he is able to canalize his urges and instincts. Man can fight against his own instincts. He is the only animal who limits from within his instinctual drives. Some domestic animals can do likewise, when their love for man comes into conflict with their animal drives. Neurotic people can breed neurotic dogs, with all their drives caught in the dog's basket.

For naked undefended man, the outer fight became an inner fight. His fighting became partly a fight against inner urges, partly against the inhibiting forces from outside. There is always a confusion of oppositely directed struggles in man.

When man has overcome sexual fear and aggression, he will be able to direct his love, that higher form of libidinous development toward the world. But when he feels defeated inwardly, through loss of love, loss of paternal defense, loss of inner capacity, he wishes to hide himself behind his aggressive fantasies. Or worse; he retakes the pattern of the insectual warrior, in order to rid himself of his depression in a primitive way. He laughs and is furious and aggressive because he is sad.

However, man is not a real fighter, or he would not have invented the perversion of destructive tools.

Homo Ludens—The Playing Man

A long youth and an eagerness to learn are not enough to transform the human animal into a civilized being. His youth must be relatively safe, so that he may learn by *playing*.

We already observe this pedagogical play in the higher animals. The larvae of the wasp must catch its prey by innate reflex, but most of the vertebrate animals exercise and train their reflexes. They create a secondary motility, which gives them greater variety in stalking and conquering their prey. The infant-phase of the animal at home in the parental nest makes this training in motor variety possible.

However, we must distinguish between playing and learning. Every higher animal experiences and learns; he finds a new exercise in every new experience. That is why many animals can be drilled so very well. In terms of biological aim, we may say that the motor patterns become more and more useful. Specific training in the parental nest is directed toward the service of a specific biological aim and satisfaction. But there is another form of movement beside that which fulfills the biological aim. Some animals are capable of "aimless play". Many baby animals play in the parental nest, though prey or enemy are not present. My dog does the same. "Come, come," I say, and he comes head over heels, bringing me the stockings he has in his corner. No archaic instinct leads him; it is the play of movement, of repetition and new movement, which gives him all kinds of satisfaction. But this is only possible when he is not attacking his competitor or eating his meal. In his play the animal is without direct biological aim, his motility is independent of innate reflexes. Human beings have the same tendency in thousand-fold varieties. Here, too, man's fetal nakedness invites him to play. Man is born naked without natural claws and weapons. He has to learn his own defenses by playing his play of strategy with artificial tools. Man has to discharge his innate aggression, because he is a naked fetus; and he has to learn to defend, because there is still danger in the world. In games and sports he finds a partial solution of this human paradox of aggression.

The motile function as such has value as we learned already. It helps to form private virtual worlds. Every movement is conducted by virtual movements, and virtual movements help to form ideas. That is why one wishes to repeat a game; it is not the aim, but the joy of motor function itself. The psychologists call it "Wiederholungszwang", the compulsion to repeat. We find it, for example, in the ornamental play of primitive peoples. Some of the roots of creative art lie in the playful repetition of a primary simple symbolic figure. Play becomes style, and style becomes an idea.

Play, handed on by the parents to the next generation, is the beginning of culture. It seeks an *active* motor function, seeks a joy in action quite different from the training of inborn reflex motility, which is pure *"reactive"* movement.

Scientific language is too dry and barren for describing the fluent crossings, from one problem to another, which arise in the beginning of play and civilization. Nearly all the essential problems of culture have their roots in these primitive attempts to overcome the rules of animal life.

As soon as mere reflexive life ceases to exist, as soon as the life which reacts only to stimuli from outside is turned toward play, with an aim of its own, a conflict arises with the outside world. In any case the new "ludicrous" attitude can only then be developed if the biological aims are secure. In this craving for security we find the roots of civilized fear, namely the fear of insecurity. All freedom to play contains a vague fear of the period of non-playing when we are again bound to our instincts. Our homesickness, our "Weltschmerz", our tendency to preserve eternally the secure nest of father and mother is part of the eternal oedipal tragedy. However, we can escape our human fear and hesitations in the highest ecstasy of creation or in the most boring game of cards!

The Quest For Safety

Civilized man is not able to hunt for his prey every day; he cannot be constantly on the alert. He has a tendency to make life safer and safer and to eternalize the infantile situation. This is one of the roots of fear inherent in every cultural being. Because man removes himself from his biological aim and makes his own laws and his own rules, there is always the risk of falling back into the old insectual attitude. Of course, it is also possible to use our play in the service of the instincts. The choice between free play and instinctual satisfaction is an ancient tragedy. Look at my dog. I call him and, wagging his tail, he is ready to play. But at the same time outside the door barks his eternal enemy and competitor in sex life. He pricks up his ears. And now his internal struggle begins—here the play and there the instinct. With a deep human sigh he goes back to his boss—tomorrow, perhaps, he will rush outdoors and follow his innate instincts.

In the choice between instinct and play lies the idea of biological freedom, the determined freedom of option between regression or progression. We see it in the play between cat and mouse. At any moment the decision can move in either of two ways: the oral instinct can be satisfied and the mouse incorporated, or the game is played and creates a new kind of satisfaction. Next day the boss finds a dead mouse on the floor.

Human beings, too, always have the freedom of this primary and archaic choice. In his table manners man plays the old game, up to the moment of the swallowing reflex. Have you forgotten how you have tried to delay swallowing when some food was wonderfully tasty? But the most beautiful game is played by the human being in the elaborate play of Eros which grew to a thousandfold cultural pattern of its own. And behind the erotic culture always remains the sexual reflex. The archaic choice between cat and mouse is turned into man's chaotic problems of love. The culture of love, the repeated play of Eros in our society is conducted in the safe harbor of marriage. Here again, the repetition creates a culture. Until the moment comes when the cat eats the mouse. This is the moment when the old aggression and destruction trouble civilization and culture. The love of Eros cannot compete with the aggression of sex.

I like this picture of the human animal, who plays continually in a safe world. This tendency toward safety is the beginning of social life. Play is only insured when the archaic instincts can be safely satisfied. This insurance policy is the protector of our culture.

In all play, there is a magic function—the recognition of the player himself, of his ego. First life acted on him; now he lives actively and places himself opposite life. Man through his play becomes aware of his errors; he is the only animal who rearranges his life again and again according to plan, or play, or emergency. Play for him is a continual challenge; he tries, he errs, he corrects and tries again.

Play is adventure; it is freedom. We never know in advance what will happen. Play is anti-instinct, for instinct is limited. As I have said, there are several ways in which play degenerates when it serves the instincts. Then it turns into routine, into destructive technique. Sport and fair play may develop into ambitious competitiveness—decent interhuman competition turn into destructive war with perfidious instruments. Insectual patterns—with help of the technique—dominate the irrational aim of fair play.

The human being is able to play and to create his own civilized world out of his play, because he has a long youth.

The Sclerotized Student

Most of us end our student days when we are less than 25 years old. Then we must develop the film which was photographed from reality. We think over and over again about the things we discovered up to then. We see that the brain without innate ideas has been filled in part with a traditional and in part with a self-discovered world. The body walks erect; it has tasted new things and has brought them into its picture of the world. For most people real play stops when they imagine themselves to be adult. Their eyes no longer look; their hands no longer feel; their ears no longer hear. Youth has passed, no verification occurs any longer. One still speaks of play, but it is only imitation. Play has turned into a pastime or a sensation or a tournament with fate (as in roulette) or a poisoned state which imitates the real ecstasy of creation or shows one's pseudo-superiority. The risk of growing and maturing is that we lose pure human functions, that we lose possibilities of expression and creation. We grow rigid and get culturally atrophic. Psychosclerosis may begin in youth. Play for the sake of play, play full of cultural tension and cultural relaxation seems too difficult for many people. Nevertheless, only this active play keeps the spirit high and the human being young. Only in highest regions of the arts and sciences does one dare to play, till in old age one arrives at that free creative play of thinking and correcting and thinking again, and the relaxed laughter, which follows when one realizes the nonsense one has created before. In spite of dictatorship and power politics, culture is only born in these regions.

In remodeling reality, in repeating its forms in a playful way, man learns to create his own world outside himself. Only man possesses an ideal world, a pure image, made only inside his own mind. He never realizes that ideal, he is always dissatisfied in his creative artistic play, but he is sure of his projected dreamworld as a stronger one than reality.

We have walked rather quickly past a few biological views. The human animal has valuable gifts: his ability to walk erect and his long youth. That is why his body became a precious instrument, with which he comes into contact with the miracles of the world and is able to carry that world into his own brain.

Straight and erect, man walks over the earth building his own world. He had to be trained to use his instruments, that is why he needed time to learn. Man has a long youth, during which—protected by his parents—he can learn most of his cultural play.

Open to all impressions, man is permitted to see the world and to experience the miracle of everything on earth. He is allowed to revel in all aspects of reality. Thus the human being matures, and life matures in him.

To remain young means to remain a student. To walk erect means to search for truth. To continue to play means to remain surprised and astonished and to revel in the developing human mind.

Man is an inquisitive animal, a persistent student, who learns by playing.

References

1. Allport, Gordon W. *A.B.C.'s of Scapegoating*. Chicago: Central Y.M.C.A. College, 1944.
2. Bacon, Francis. *Novum Organon*. In: Bacon's Works. London: George Newness Ltd., 1892.
3. Bleuler. *Lehrbuch der Psychiatrie*. Berlin: Springer Verlag, 1920.
4. Bolk, L. *Brain and Culture*. Amsterdam, 1925.
5. Bolk, L. *Das Problem der Menschwerdung*. Jena, 1926.
6. Charles Madge & Tom Harrison. *Britain by Mass Observation*. London: Penguin Books, Ltd., 1939.
7. Ferenczi, S. *Stages in the Development of the Sense of Reality*, in Outline of Psychoanalysis. New York: The New Library, 1924.
8. Hitler, A. *Mein Kampf*, New York: Stackpole Sons, 1939.
9. James, William. *The Varieties of Religious Experience*. New York: The New Library, 1902.
10. Jung, C. G. *The Relations Between the Ego and the Unconscious*. The Hague: N. V. Servire, 1937.
    Psychology of the Unconscious. New York: Moffat, Yard and Company, 1916.
11. Le Bon, Gustave. *The Psychology of Peoples*. Paris: F. Alcan, 1923.
12. Levy-Bruhl. *Primitive Mentality*. London: G. Allen and Unwin, Ltd., 1923.
13. Meerloo, A. M. *Uber Das Halluzinieren*. Z. Neur. 152. Berlin: Springer, 1935.
14. Meerloo, A. M. *Blacksheep, Scapegoats and Werewolves*. Review 46. London, 1946.
15. Meerloo, A. M. *Aftermath of Peace*. New York: Intern. Universities Press, 1947.
16. Meerloo, A. M. *Psychological Experiences in a Small Army*. Psychiatric Quarterly. Vol. 21. Part I, 1947.
17. Scheler, Max. *Die Stellung des Menschen im Kosmos*. Darmstadt, 1928.
18. Stimson, H. L. *On Active Service*. New York: Harper & Bros., 1948.
19. Von Monakow, C. and Mourgue, A. *Neurobiologie de l'Hallucination*. Brussels, 1932.
20. Werner, Heinz. *Comparative Psychology of Mental Development*. New York: Harper & Bros. 1940.
21. Van der Hoop. *Bewusztseinstypen*. Bern: Huber Verlag, 1937.

ADDITIONAL REFERENCES ON THE SUBJECT

Alexander, Franz. *Our Age of Unreason*. New York: J. B. Lippincott Company, 1942.

Bally, G. *Die Fruhkindliche Motorik*. Imago. 1933.

Baschwitz, Kurt. *Der Massenwahn*. Munchen, 1924. *Du und die Masse*. Feikema, Coardson & Co. Amsterdam, 1938.

Benedict, Ruth. *Patterns of Culture*. New York: Houghton Mifflin Co., 1934.

Bierens, De Haan. *Animal Language in its Relation to that of Man*. Biological Review, 1930. Scientia, Vol. 55, 1934.

Blondel, Charles. Ch. *Introduction a la Psychologie Collective*. Paris: A Colin, 1941.

Boas, Franz. *The Mind of Primitive Man*. New York: The Macmillan Company, 1939.

Race, Language and Culture. New York: The Macmillan Company, 1940.

Brend, William A. *Foundations of Human Conflict*. London: Kegan Paul, 1947.

Buytendyk. *Het Spel van Mensch En Dier*. Amsterdam, 1932.

Chase, Stuart. *The Tyranny of Words*. New York: Harcourt, Brace, 1938.

Crawshay-Williams, R. *The Comfort of Unreason*. London: Kegan Paul, 1947.

Dewey, John. *How We Think*. New York: D. C. Heath & Co., 1933.

Frazer, J. G. *The Golden Bough*. London: Macmillan & Co., 1900.

Freud, Sigmund. *A General Introduction to Psychoanalysis*. Tr. by Joan Riviere. New York: Liveright, 1935.

Freud, Sigmund. *Civilization and Its Discontents*. London: L. & V. Woolf, 1930.

Freud, Sigmund. *Group Psychology and the Analysis of the Ego*. London: Hogarth Press, 1922.

Freud, Sigmund. *Totem and Taboo*. New York: Moffatt, Yard and Co., 1918.

Freud, Sigmund. *Beyond the Pleasure Principle*. London: Hogarth Press, 1922.

Friedmann, Max. *Ueber Wahnideeen im Voelkerleben*. J. F. Borgmann, 1901.

Fromm, Erich. *Escape from Freedom*. New York: Farrar and Rinehart, 1941.

Goldstein, Kurt. *Human Nature*. Cambridge, Massachusetts: Harvard University Press, 1947.

Groos, Karl. *Die Spiele der Menschen*. New York: D. Appleton & Co., 1901.

Hortega, Y. Gasset. *The Rebellion of the Masses*. The Hague, Leopold, My. 1936.

Kardiner, A. *The Psychological Frontiers of Society*. New York: Columbia University Press, 1944.

Kasanin, J. S. *Language and Thought in Schizophrenia*. Berkeley: University of California Press, 1944.

Koffka, Kurt. *The Growth of the Mind*. London: K. Paul, Trench, Trubner & Co. Ltd., 1924.

Kohler, Wolfgang. *Intelligenzprufungen an Menschenaffen*. Berlin: Springer, 1921.

Lasswell, Harold D. *Propaganda Technique in the World War*. New York: Peter Smith, 1938.

Lasswell, Harold D. *Power and Personality*. New York: W. W. Norton and Co., 1948.

McDougall, W. *Introduction to Social Psychology*. Boston: J. W. Luce Co., 1909.

Meerloo, A. M. *Total War and the Human Mind*. New York: Intern. Universities Press, 1946.

Murphy, and Newcomb. *Experimental Social Psychology*. New York: Harper & Bros., 1937.

Neurath, Otto. *Modern Man in the Making*. New York: A. A. Knopf, 1939.

Petersen. *Ueber die Biologischen Grundlagen der Stellung des Menschen*. Klinische Wschr. Berlin, 1928.

Piaget, Jean. *The Language and Thought of the Child*. New York: Harcourt, Brace and Company, 1926.

Porteus, S. D. *Primitive Intelligence and Environment*. New York: Macmillan Company, 1937.

Radin, Paul. *Primitive Man as Philosopher*. New York: D. Appleton & Company, 1927.

Reik, Theodor. *Ritual: Psychoanalytic Studies*. London: L. & V. Woolf, 1931.

Rivers, W. H. R. *Instinct and the Unconscious*. London, 1922.

Schilder, Paul. *The Psychology of Schizophrenia*. The Psychoanalytic Review, Vol. 26, 1939.

Schneirla, T. C. *Problems in the Biopsychology of Social Organization*. Journ. of Abn. and Soc. Psychology, Vol. 41, 1946.

Stebbing, L. Susan. *Thinking to Some Purpose*. London: Penguin Books, Ltd., 1939.

Thouless, R. H. *Straight Thinking in War Time*. London, 1942.

Trotter, W. *Instincts of the Herd in Peace and War*. London: T. F. Unwin, Ltd., 1916.

Uexkuell, J. V. *Umwelt und Innenwelt der Tiere*. Berlin, 1921.

Young, Kimball. *Handbook of Social Psychology*. London: Kegan Paul, 1946.

Lightning Source UK Ltd.
Milton Keynes UK
UKHW010651140821
388823UK00005B/1141